D1608273

Sunburst

William K. Durr
Jean M. LePere
Bess Niehaus
Barbara York

CONSULTANT Paul McKee

HOUGHTON MIFFLIN COMPANY • Boston

Atlanta • Dallas • Geneva, Illinois • Hopewell, New Jersey • Palo Alto • Toronto

Acknowledgments

For each of the selections listed below, grateful acknowledgment is made for permission to adapt and/or reprint copyrighted material, as follows:

"And Hippos Too!" by Eunice deChazeau. Reprinted from *Ranger Rick's Nature Magazine* by permission of the publisher, the National Wildlife Federation.

"Andy and Mr. Wagner." From *Andy and Mr. Wagner*, by Gina Bell. Copyright © 1957 by Abingdon Press.

"The Case of the Stolen Code Book." Taken from *The Case of the Stolen Code Book* by Barbara Rinkoff. Text © 1971 by Barbara Rinkoff; illustrations © 1971 by Leonard Shortall. Used by permission of Crown Publishers, Inc.

"Cradle Song," from *The American Rhythm, Studies and Reexpressions of Amerindian Songs* by Mary Austin. Reprinted with permission of Houghton Mifflin Company.

"Do You Have the Time, Lydia?" From the book *Do You Have the Time, Lydia?* by Evaline Ness. Illustrated by the author. Copyright © 1971 by Evaline Ness. Published by E. P. Dutton & Co., Inc. and used with their permission. British rights granted by The Bodley Head.

"Eskimo Chant," reprinted by permission of William Collins+World Publishing Co., Inc., from *Beyond the High Hills, A Book of Eskimo Poems* edited by Knud Rasmussen. Copyright © 1961 by William Collins+World Publishing Co., Inc.

"Follow the Wind." *Follow the Wind* by Alvin Tresselt is reprinted by permission of Lothrop, Lee & Shepard Co., Inc. Copyright 1950 by Lothrop, Lee & Shepard Co., Inc.

"Gabrielle and Selena." *Gabrielle and Selena*, © 1968, by Peter Desbarats. Reprinted, with slight adaptations, by permission of Harcourt Brace Jovanovich, Inc. Also reprinted by permission of Collins-Knowlton-Wing, Inc. Copyright © 1968 by Peter Desbarats.

"Ginger's·Upstairs Pet." From *Ginger's Upstairs Pet* by John Ryckman, reprinted with the permission of Garrard Publishing Co., Champaign, Illinois. Copyright 1971 by Thomas Nelson & Sons (Canada), Limited.

"Giraffes." From *The Raucous Auk* by Mary Ann Hoberman. Text Copyright © 1973 by Mary Ann Hoberman. Reprinted by permission of The Viking Press, Inc.

"Girls Can Be Anything." From the book *Girls Can Be Anything* by Norma Klein. Illustrated by Roy Doty. Text copyright © 1973 by Norma Klein. Published by E. P. Dutton & Co., Inc. and used with their permission.

"Impossible, Possum," by Ellen Conford. Text copyright © 1971 by Ellen Conford. From *Impossible, Possum* by Ellen Conford, by permission of Little, Brown and Co.

"maggie and milly and molly and may." From *95 Poems*, © 1958, by e. e. cummings. Reprinted by permission of Harcourt Brace Jovanovich, Inc. and Granada Publishing Limited.

"Mrs. Brownish Beetle." From *Up the Windy Hill* by Aileen Fisher. Reprinted by permission of Scott, Foresman and Company.

"Parking Lot." From *That Was Summer* by Marci Ridlon, published by Follett Publishing Company. Reprinted by permission of the author.

"Play Street — Area Closed." Taken from *This Street's for Me!* by Lee Bennett Hopkins. © 1970 by Lee Bennett Hopkins. Used by permission of Crown Publishers, Inc.

"The Porcupine," reprinted with permission of The Macmillan Co., Inc. from *Toucans Two and Other Poems* by Jack Prelutsky. Copyright © 1967, 1970 by Jack Prelutsky. Published in Great Britain under the title "Zoo Doings." British rights granted by Hamish Hamilton Ltd.

"A Race," by Mrs. Molesworth. From *The Book of Nonsense* by Roger Lancelyn Green. Copyright © 1956 by J. M. Dent & Sons, Ltd. The Children's Illustrated Classics. Reprinted by permission of the publishers, E. P. Dutton & Co., Inc. and J. M. Dent & Sons Ltd., Publishers.

"Red Fox and the Hungry Tiger." Adapted from *Red Fox and the Hungry Tiger*, text © 1962, by Paul Anderson. A Young Scott Book, by permission of Addison-Wesley Publishing Company.

"Robert, Who Is Often a Stranger to Himself," from *Bronzeville Boys and Girls* by Gwendolyn Brooks. Text copyright © 1956 by Gwendolyn Brooks Blakely. Reprinted by permission of Harper & Row, Publishers, Inc.

"The Secret," from *Is Somewhere Always Far Away?* by Leland B. Jacobs. Copyright © 1967 by Leland B. Jacobs. Reprinted by permission of Holt, Rinehart and Winston, Inc.

"The Secret Hiding Place." Reprinted by permission of The World Publishing Company from *Secret Hiding Place* by Rainey Bennett. Copyright © 1960 by Rainey Bennett. British rights granted by Blackie & Son Limited.

"Spinning Song." Text copyright © 1969 by Zilpha Keatley Snyder. From *Today is Saturday*. Used by permission of Atheneum Publishers.

"Twelve Years, Twelve Animals." From *Twelve Years, Twelve Animals* by Yoshiko Samuel. Copyright © 1972 by Abingdon Press.

"A Window." From *Photographs and Poems by Sioux Children*, published by Indian Arts·and Crafts Board, United States Department of the Interior. Reprinted by permission of Mr. Arthur Amiotte.

"The Wizard of Wallaby Wallow." Adaptation of *The Wizard of Wallaby Wallow*, copyright © 1971 by Jack Kent. Reprinted by permission of Parents' Magazine Press.

Printed in the U.S.A.
ISBN: 0-395-20408-9

Contents

MOON GLOW

Daybreak

The Secret Hiding Place

by Rainey Bennett

Little Hippo was the pet of all the hippos. Every morning the big hippos waited for him to get up so they could take care of him.

"Sh-Sh," they whispered. "Little Hippo is sleeping."

Every morning the big hippos would bring Little Hippo his breakfast. Then they all sat down to watch Little Hippo eat.

7

One morning Little Hippo felt cross.
"I don't want any breakfast," he said. "I wish
the hippos wouldn't watch everything I do.
I wish I could be by myself once in a while."

"Don't eat so fast," Big Charles said.

All the hippos went along when Big Charles
took Little Hippo for his morning walk.

"We will take care of you,"
said Big Charles.

But Little Hippo didn't want all the hippos
to come. He wanted to go looking
around by himself. What fun is a walk
with nineteen hippos?

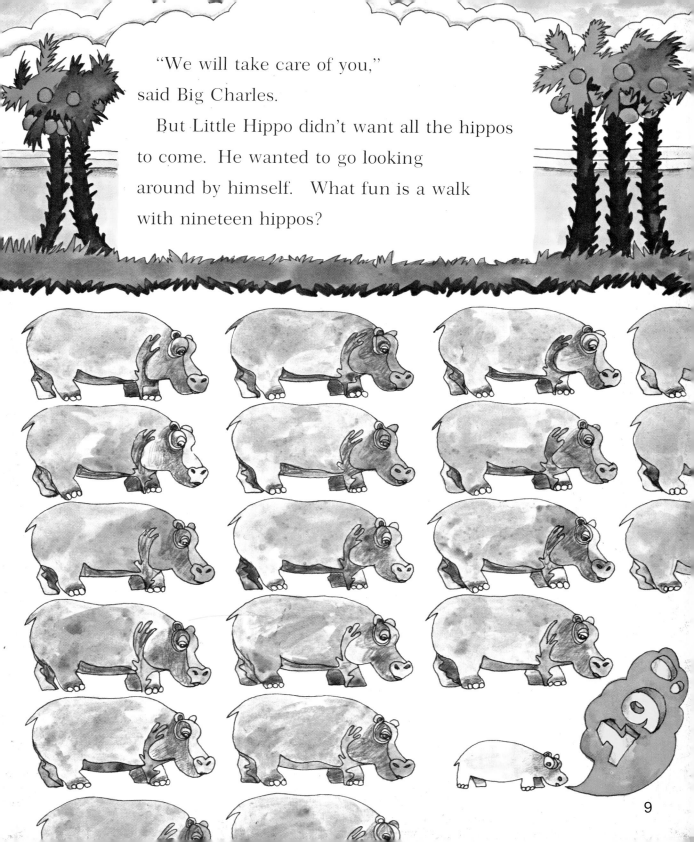

Without even saying, "Excuse me, please,"
Little Hippo ran to some bushes.

"Stop, Little Hippo," Big Charles
shouted. "Birds nest there.

10

"Don't go in the tall grass where zebras hide. Do you want to get stripes?"

Little Hippo stopped to look at an ostrich that was hiding its head.

"Come away, Little Hippo," Big Charles shouted. "He thinks he's hiding."

When Big Charles got to Little Hippo, he was hot and angry. "That's a chameleon's house. Come away this minute!" he puffed.

"Don't you know better than to go looking into secret places?" Big Charles asked.

Everyone in the jungle had a hiding place, it seemed, but Little Hippo. The tiger had a place in the tall grass. Monkeys went up in trees. Even the elephant was nearly hidden by leaves as big as his ears.

14

"You're lucky," Little Hippo told the turtle. "You have your hiding place with you. What's it like inside?"

"It's dark," said the turtle.

15

What Kind of Place?

Little Hippo was still cross at lunch. But later that afternoon, after he'd had some sleep, there was a big surprise.

"We will play hide-and-seek," Big Charles said. "I will be IT." He stood by a tree and started to count. "I will count to five hundred by fives," said Big Charles.

5..10...15..20..25

"Now!" Little Hippo whispered. "Now I can find a hiding place of my very own."

He ran to the flowering trees.

"Little Hippo, Little Hippo, come hide with us," some Hippos called.

But Little Hippo wanted his own hiding place. "I'll hide in the river," he thought.

"Little Hippo, Little Hippo, hide with us," some other hippos cried.

"Oh, no," Little Hippo said to himself.

The lion laughed when he saw Little Hippo trying to crawl under a rock.

"Silly hippo," he said. "That's no place to hide. Follow me. You can hide in my cave."

"Are we almost there?" asked Little Hippo.

"Here we are," said the lion. "Make yourself at home."

Then he went hunting for something to eat and left Little Hippo all alone.

The dark cave was full of funny noises.

"I'm scared," said Little Hippo. "I don't want to be alone this much."

Little Hippo was so scared that he ran out of the cave.

He ran for a long, long time. At last
he stopped running.

"I can't run any more," he puffed.

Just then the chameleon put its head
out of its house.

"Why, hello, Little Hippo," he said.
"What are you doing here?"

"I'm lost," said Little Hippo.

"You're lost?" said the chameleon.
"Follow me!"

He took Little Hippo to the top of a small hill.
"Now, look, Little Hippo!"

And there right below him was Big Charles.
He and all the other hippos were looking
for something. "Little Hippo, come out,"
they called, pushing through the grass.

"Come out, come out, wherever you are!"
they shouted, looking under rocks.

But not one of them thought of looking up.

Little Hippo laughed and laughed. "They'll
never find me here," he said. "They don't see
me, and I'm right up here."

"Home free, home free," Little Hippo shouted as he ran up to Big Charles.

All the big hippos were so happy to see him! They shouted and stamped their feet.

"Where did you hide, Little Hippo? We looked everywhere," said Big Charles.

But Little Hippo didn't tell him. He just smiled because he knew that the big hippos would always look everywhere but up. And he never told anyone about his secret hiding place where he could be alone, but not too alone.

Animal Coloring

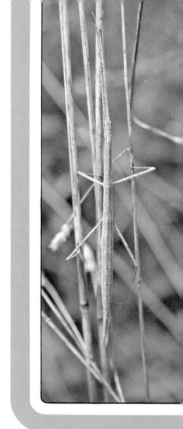

Have you ever heard a bird singing in a tree, but when you looked up you couldn't see the bird? Have you ever picked up a leaf or a twig, only to find it was a small, living insect?

It is possible for you not to have seen the bird, or not to have known that the twig was an insect because of the coloring of the bird and the insect.

Many animals have coloring which helps them hide from danger.

Look at the picture below and see how many baby birds you can find in the nest.

The chameleon is well known for being able to change its color. If the chameleon is on a leaf, this animal can change its color to match the leaf. If it is on the ground, the chameleon can change its color to match the ground. One kind of chameleon can even change its color to match your hand as you hold it.

Some fish can hide by changing their color. Look at the picture below and see if you can find the fish.

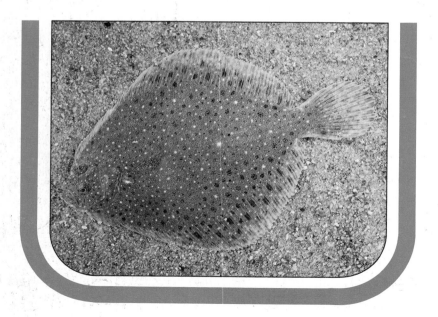

Did you ever hear a frog croak and then try to find the frog? Maybe you could see the frog only when it jumped into the water, or when it jumped out of your way as you walked through the grass.

It is possible that you couldn't find the frog because of its color.

Many frogs are very well hidden because of their coloring. Look at the picture on this page and see if you can find the frog.

Some animals change color at different times of the year. The snowshoe rabbit is one of those animals. The snowshoe rabbit is brown in the spring and summer. This makes it hard to see the rabbit as it runs across the ground. In the fall and winter the snowshoe rabbit's color changes to white. Then the rabbit is hard to see against the snow.

Look at the two pictures of the snowshoe rabbit and notice how its color changes at different times of the year.

The next time you are outdoors, notice how the coloring of some animals helps them to hide from danger.

Ginger's Upstairs Pet

by John Ryckman

Ginger was a little girl who lived in a house
with lots of steps. One day Ginger
came down the steps from her bedroom.

She called, "Mother, may I have a piece
of cake?" But her mother didn't answer.

Ginger looked all around. "Mother
must be downstairs," said Ginger.
"I'll go and see."

Ginger found her mother. "Mother,
may I have a piece of cake?"

"Yes," said Ginger's mother,
"but don't eat too much."

"Oh, it's not for me," said Ginger.
"It's for my new pet."

"I think the cake is for you,"
said Ginger's mother. "You don't have a pet."

"But I do have a pet," said Ginger.
"He's a funny pet." Ginger went up
to the kitchen. She cut a piece of cake.
She took it up to her room.

After a while she came down again.
Her mother was in the kitchen.

"Mother, may I have some apples?"
Ginger asked.

"Didn't your pet like the cake?"
asked Ginger's mother.

"Oh yes," said Ginger, "but now I think
he wants some apples."

Ginger's mother said, "I think your pet
is a little girl named Ginger. I think
she eats too much."

"I do have a pet," said Ginger.
"He's very hungry." Ginger took five apples.
She went back up to her room.

It wasn't long before Ginger came
back down again. This time her mother
was in the living room. "Mother, may I have
some carrots?" she asked.

"Don't tell me your pet wants to eat
some carrots," said Ginger's mother.

"Yes, I think he does," answered Ginger.

Ginger's mother said, "Your pet eats cake. Your pet eats apples. Your pet wants carrots. I think your pet must be a pig."

Ginger laughed. "Oh no," she said. "He's not a pig. But he's a funny pet. He's still hungry." She got the carrots and went upstairs.

Soon she came down again. "My pet
wants some milk," she said.

"Is your pet a kitten?" asked Ginger's mother.

"No, my pet isn't a kitten. But I think
he'd like some milk," said Ginger.

Her mother said, "I think you're eating
all that food. And I think you'll get fat."

"Oh, no, I won't get fat," said Ginger.
"And my pet won't get fat. He's a very big pet."

She went up to her room with the milk.
Down she came again.

"What does your pet want this time?"
asked her mother.

"I think he wants some green leaves,"
answered Ginger.

Her mother was surprised. "Green leaves?"
her mother said. "Is your pet a rabbit?"

"No, he's not a rabbit," laughed Ginger.
"He's much bigger than a rabbit."

"We don't have any green leaves,"
said Ginger's mother. "I think I'll come up
and see your pet."

Ginger and her mother went up the stairs.
They went into Ginger's room. There was
Ginger's pet.

"Where did you find him?" asked Ginger's
mother.

"I didn't find him," said Ginger.
"He just came to the window. I think
he wants to stay with us."

Just then there was a knock on the front
door. "I'll get it," cried Ginger.

Ginger ran downstairs. She opened the door.
There stood a man.

"I'm from the zoo," the man said.
"A big giraffe has gotten out of the zoo.
We think he came this way. Have you seen him?"

"Yes," said Ginger, "he's my pet. I'm feeding
him cake and apples and carrots and milk.
But I think he wants some green leaves."

"Where is he?" asked the man.

"He's at the back of our house. He's
looking in my window," answered Ginger.
"I think he's waiting for me to get
some green leaves."

"We have lots of green leaves at the zoo,"
said the man. "We'll take him back there."

Ginger and her mother watched the man
take the giraffe away. "Your pet will be happy
at the zoo," said Ginger's mother. "They
have lots of green leaves for him."

"But he'll miss the cake and apples and milk,"
said Ginger. "And he'll miss me, too."

"We can go to see him in the zoo,"
said her mother.

"When?" asked Ginger.

"Tomorrow," answered her mother.

"Great," said Ginger. She went upstairs.
She went into her room and closed the window.
Soon she came down again. "I'm hungry,"
Ginger said.

"I know why you're hungry," her mother said.
"It's all the running up and down stairs.
Come with me and we'll see what we can find
in the kitchen."

Robert, Who Is Often a Stranger to Himself

Do you ever look in the looking-glass
And see a stranger there?
A child you know and do not know,
Wearing what you wear?

Gwendolyn Brooks

Thinking the Right Meaning

PLEASE LEAVE NOW.

THE LEAVES HAVE TURNED YELLOW NOW.

GROAN.

ONLY IF HE TURNS YELLOW.

WILL HE LEAVE NOW, MOM?

Look at the word *leaves* in these sentences:

I hope he **leaves** soon.

The **leaves** have turned yellow now.

You can see that the word *leaves* does not have the same meaning in the two sentences. But you knew what meaning was right for each one because the other words told you which meaning would make good sense there.

Many words have more than one meaning. That's why you will often need to be sure that you think the right meaning for a word.

If the first meaning you think of doesn't make sense, you can almost always be sure it is not the right meaning. The meaning you think of must make sense in the sentence.

Use what the other words in these sentences are saying to help you know what the meaning of each word in heavy black letters is:

Daddy said he would **park** the car.

We ate our lunch in the **park.**

Jill had the ball in her **hand.**

Will you **hand** me the milk?

I told my dog to get the **stick.**

Can the picture **stick** on the wall?

Come and **watch** me play ball.

What time does your **watch** show?

I wanted to see the **show.**

Will you **show** me your new coat?

MRS. BROWNISH BEETLE

When it was October
and a hard frost came,
Mrs. Brownish Beetle
(I don't know her other name)
said: "Dear me, it's chilly,"
said: "My coat is thin,"
said: "Land sakes, I'd better find
    a place to cuddle in."

So Mrs. Brownish Beetle,
after several tries,
found a hole beneath a stone
that was a beetle's size,
and said: "Oh my, how lucky,"
said: "How very nice,"
said: "I'll snuggle down away
    from the wind and snow and ice.

"I'll set my clock at April,"
Mrs. Beetle said,
"I'll wind it up and put it here
beside my little bed."
So Mrs. Brownish Beetle
(I don't know her other name)
nestled down and went to sleep
and slept till April came.

Aileen Fisher

43

ANDY and Mr. WAGNER

BY GINA BELL

Andy Brooks sat on the front steps thinking. He was thinking about a dog because he wanted a dog.

Andy had wanted a dog for a long time. And he knew just what kind of dog he wanted.

His dog would be a beautiful dog! Not too big and not too little! He would have big brown eyes and a reddish-brown coat. Best of all, he would have a long fluffy tail.

Andy even had a name for his dog. He would be called Mr. Wagner. Mr. Wagner was Andy's friend who owned the toy shop.

Suddenly Andy jumped up and ran into the house.

"Mother!" he called. "When can I have Mr. Wagner?"

Mrs. Brooks looked at Andy. "I don't have time to take care of a dog now. When little Susie is older, I'll have more time. Then maybe you can have your dog."

"But I'll take care of my dog," Andy said. "I'll take care of him all by myself."

"Well, we can't be sure of that," said Mrs. Brooks. "You will just have to wait."

"May I go down to the pet store and look at the dogs?" Andy asked. "May I go see if Mr. Wagner is there now? Susie is getting bigger every day."

"All right, run along," his mother said. "But don't stay too long."

In the pet shop window, Andy saw three dogs.

To each dog Andy said, "You're not
Mr. Wagner. You're almost the color
of Mr. Wagner, but Mr. Wagner's tail will be
longer and fluffier than yours. You're not as
smart as Mr. Wagner. Mr. Wagner will be
the smartest dog in the world."

Andy started home. "I wish I could have
Mr. Wagner soon," he said.

He was still thinking about Mr. Wagner
when a little dog ran up to him. It was a little
yellow dog with black spots and a short
stump-of-a-tail.

"Hi, doggy," Andy said and kept right
on walking. Soon he was in his own
front yard.

"Andrew!" It was his mother calling. She was standing by the door. "Andrew Brooks, where did you get that dog?"

"What dog?" Andy asked.

"That little yellow and black dog behind you," his mother answered.

Andy looked around. There behind
him was the little yellow and black dog,
wagging its stump-of-a-tail.

"I don't know where he came from," Andy
said. "I saw him down the street. He must
have followed me home."

"Make him go away," said Mrs. Brooks. "He
can't stay here."

"Go on," said Andy. "Go on home. You're
not my dog. You're not my Mr. Wagner.
Go on home."

The dog looked at Andy. Then it turned and
went off down the street.

The next morning as Andy walked to school, he was thinking about Mr. Wagner. It seemed as if his beautiful dog were right beside him. Suddenly Andy looked down. A dog was right beside him, but it was the little yellow and black dog. Its stump-of-a-tail was wagging back and forth.

Andy smiled at the dog. "You are a nice little dog," he said. "But you don't belong to me. Go on home." Andy walked on without looking back.

At the corner Mike, the police officer, stopped him.

"I didn't know you had a dog, Andy," he said. "You really should give him more to eat. He looks hungry."

Andy looked down.

"That's not my dog," he said. "I want a dog, but I don't have one yet. My dog is going to be beautiful! He'll be reddish-brown, and he'll have a long fluffy tail."

"That dog's no beauty," the police officer said, "but he seems to think he's your dog."

"I know," said Andy. "But he's just following me."

When Andy had crossed the street, he
looked down at the little dog.

"You do look hungry," Andy said. He
opened his lunchbox and took out a cookie.

"Here," he said. "Here is a cookie for you."

The little dog ate the cookie. Then it looked
up at Andy and wagged its stump-of-a-tail.

"Now I have to go to school, and you have
to go home. Go on." Andy ran on to school.

Not My Dog

"Andrew Brooks!" cried the teacher as Andy came into the room. "When did we start bringing dogs to school?"

Andy looked around. The little yellow and black dog was right behind him.

"He isn't my dog, Miss Smith," said Andy. "He just followed me here."

"Well, he seems to think he's your dog," said Miss Smith. "Please take him outside."

Andy took the little dog to the door.

"Go home," he said. "Dogs don't belong in school. Any smart dog should know that. And you're not my dog anyway."

The little yellow and black dog looked up at Andy. Then it started slowly up the street.

After school Andy walked home
with his two friends Bob and Steve. On the way
he told them about Mr. Wagner.

"My Mr. Wagner will be beautiful," he said.
"And he will be waiting for me every day when
I come home."

Soon the boys came to Andy's yard. The little
yellow and black dog ran up, wagging
its stump-of-a-tail. It jumped up and down.
It barked. It ran round and round.

"Is *that* your Mr. Wagner?" Bob asked.

"No, he's not my dog. I don't know who he belongs to."

"Maybe he doesn't belong to anyone," Steve said, as the little dog sniffed at their feet.

"Maybe he doesn't," said Andy thoughtfully.

When the boys had gone, Andy and the little dog ran all around the yard. Suddenly the dog picked up something. Andy ran to see what it was. But the little dog was too fast for him. It ran to the porch and put the something down.

"Mother, Mother!" Andy called. "The little dog found your glove!"

Mrs. Brooks came to the door.

"Why, so he did," she cried.

"I've been looking for that glove all week. It was smart of the little dog to find it.

"Do you know, Andy, that dog looks hungry. Give him something to eat."

Andy went to the kitchen and got some food for the dog. When he put the food down outside, the dog ran to it. In a few minutes the food was gone.

"Now, do make him go away," Mrs. Brooks said. "He can't stay here."

"I'll try," said Andy. "But he seems to think he belongs here."

"Make him go away," said Mrs. Brooks.

"Go on!" Andy told the little dog.

Slowly the little dog walked off.

That evening Andy heard the doorbell. He went to see who was there. On the porch stood Mr. Peters, who lived next door.

"Keep that dog of yours in your yard," he said. "He was digging in my garden."

"I don't have a dog," said Andy. "I want one. But I don't have one yet."

"I mean that little yellow and black dog!" said Mr. Peters. "I see him around here all the time."

"Oh, him!" said Andy. "He's not my dog. Really he isn't."

"Well, I don't care who he belongs to," said Mr. Peters, turning away. "Keep him out of my garden."

"That dog again! I don't know what we're going to do," said Mrs. Brooks.

"I can't make him go away," answered Andy.

Mr. Brooks looked up from his paper. "We must do something about that dog!"

The next morning while the Brooks were sitting at the breakfast table, the milkman called to them. "Nice dog you have there!" he said.

Andy and his mother went out on the porch.

"You're right," Mrs. Brooks said. "He is nice."

"Friendly little dog, too," said the milkman as he walked away.

Mrs. Brooks looked at Andy. "What are we going to do with this dog? He just will not go away."

"I think he likes the food I gave him," said Andy. "He's a smart dog."

The little yellow and black dog looked up at Andy and wagged its stump-of-a-tail.

"He seems to know what we're saying," said Mrs. Brooks. "He is smart. He found my glove."

"Yes," said Andy. "And he thinks he's my dog."

"But he must belong to someone,"
said Mrs. Brooks. "We'll try to find out
if anyone has lost a dog."

"If he doesn't belong to someone, may I keep
him?" asked Andy.

"Well, maybe you should have a dog, Andy.
Will you take care of him all by yourself?"
asked Mrs. Brooks.

"Oh, yes, yes," said Andy. "You'll never
have to do a thing for him."

Andy grabbed the little dog and hugged
him. The little dog's tail wagged back and
forth. It went so fast that Andy could
hardly see it.

"If he doesn't belong to anyone, what are you
going to call him?" laughed Mrs. Brooks.

"Why, Mr. Wagner," said Andy. "I always
said I'd call my dog Mr. Wagner."

Mr. Wagner snuggled close to Andy.
Back and forth, back and forth wagged
his little stump-of-a-tail.

Using the Alphabet A to Z

What would you think if you were looking for Room 5 and found Room 4? You'd think that Room 5 must be the next room, wouldn't you? That's because we think of the numbers as coming in the order of 1, 2, 3, 4, 5. We use that order to help us find things.

We use letters in much the same way. We think of *A* as the first letter, *B* coming next, and then *C*. We put all the letters into an order that we call the **alphabet.**

ABCDEFGHIJKLMNOPQRSTUVWXYZ

We use the alphabet to put things in order so that they will be easy to find when we need them. Think how hard it would be to find someone's number in a telephone book if names in that book hadn't been placed in the order of the alphabet.

TIMBER!

IS IT YOURS OR MINE?

HELLO, MY NAME IS JACK.

Let's see if you can place names in the order
of the alphabet. Here are five names:

Can you put those names in the order
of the alphabet? Do any of the names begin
with A? Do any begin with B? The first name
on your list should be *Beth*, shouldn't it?

What letter comes after *B* in the alphabet?
Do any of the names begin with that letter?
Does any name begin with the next letter
of the alphabet? *Dick* should be the next name
on your list, shouldn't it?

Now think how the other names should
be listed. If you need to do so,
look at the alphabet.

Here are some animal names:

ostrich   *giraffe*   elephant
bear   zebra   fox

    See if you can list those names in the order
of the alphabet.

    Do you know the order of the letters
in the alphabet now? You will need to know
that order well to find what you want
in some books.

Say Cheese.

A Race

A Daisy and a Buttercup
  Agreed to have a race,
A Squirrel was to be the judge
  A mile off from the place.

The Squirrel waited patiently
  Until the day was done —
Perhaps he is there waiting still,
  You see — they couldn't run.

Mrs. Molesworth

67

Girls
Can Be
Anything

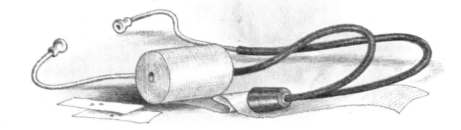

by Norma Klein

"Now we will play Hospital," said Adam Sobel.
"I will be the doctor. You will be the nurse."

Adam Sobel was Marina's best friend at school.
They went home on the bus together. They were
the only ones in their room who could do
the lion puzzle and get all the pieces together.
Most of the time Marina liked the games
Adam thought up, but this time she said,
"I want to be the doctor, too."

"You can't be doctor if I'm doctor," Adam said.

"Why not?" said Marina.

"There can't be two doctors," Adam said.

"So, you be the nurse and I'll be doctor,"
Marina said.

"That's not the way it goes," Adam said.
He was already putting on the white doctor suit
that was in the box. "Girls are always nurses
and boys are always doctors."

"Why is that?" said Marina.

"That's just the way it is," Adam said.
"Could I have the stethoscope, please, Nurse?"

That night Marina told her father at supper, "I don't like Adam Sobel at all."

"Oh?" Father said. "I thought he used to be your best friend."

"He used to be," Marina said, "but you know what he said today?"

"What?" asked Father.

"He said girls can't be doctors. They have to be just nurses."

"Well, that's just plain silly!" her father said. "Of course they can be doctors."

"They can?" asked Marina.

"Certainly they can," Father answered.
"Why, your Aunt Rosa is a doctor. You know that."

"But is she a real one?" Marina said.

"She sure is, as real as they come," Father said.

"Does she work in a hospital and have a white suit?" Marina wanted to know.

"She does," Father said. "She works in the very hospital where you were born. You know what she does there?"

"What?" said Marina.

"She's a surgeon," Father said. "That's hard work, you know."

The next day at school, Marina said to Adam,
"I have an aunt who's a doctor. She's a surgeon."

"Is she a real doctor?" Adam wanted to know.

"Of course she's real," Marina said. "She
comes to our house for supper. She even has
a white suit. Lots of women are doctors.
I might be one. I might be one that takes care
of animals. I could have my own hospital and dogs
and cats would come to see me and I would make
them better," Marina said. "That's
the kind of doctor I want to be."

"I don't even want to be a doctor," Adam said.

"What do you want to be?" asked Marina.

"I think I want to be a pilot," Adam said.

"You mean, you'd have your own airplane
and fly it from place to place?"

"Yes," Adam said. "Why don't we play
airplane right now?"

"O. K.," said Marina. "How do we do it?"

"Well," said Adam, "this is the plane
and I sit in front driving."

"What do I do?" said Marina.

"You're the stewardess," Adam said. "You
walk around in back and give people drinks."

So Marina took some cookies and milk
and walked around and gave them
to all the people on the plane. She always
asked them first what they wanted.
After a while, she went over to where Adam was
and asked, "What are you doing?"

"I'm still driving the plane," Adam said.
"Oh! Oh! Here we come! . . . It might be
a crash landing! . . . Better look out!"

"You know what?" Marina said.

"What?" said Adam, who was keeping his eyes
on the place where the plane had to land.

"I think I want to be a pilot," Marina said.

"You can't be a pilot," Adam said.

"If I want to, I can," Marina said.

"Girls can't be pilots," Adam said.
"They have to be stewardesses."

"But that's dull," said Marina. And she
went off and began to drive her own plane.

That night in bed Marina said to her mother, "Adam Sobel is so bad."

"Is he?" her mother said. "What did he do?"

"He said girls can't drive planes," Marina said. "He said they have to be stewardesses."

"That's not true," Mother said.

"Then, how come he said it?" Marina asked.

"Maybe he didn't know," Mother answered. "There was a picture of a woman in the paper just the other day, and she's been flying her own plane for nineteen years."

"Does she fly with people in it?" Marina asked.

"Of course!" said Mother.

"Does she fly it all by herself?" Marina said.

"Well, she has a co-pilot," Mother said. "Pilots always have co-pilots to help them."

"Mommy?"

"Yes, dear."

"If I was a pilot, would you and Daddy fly with me in my plane?"

"We certainly would."

"Would I be a good pilot, do you think?" Marina asked.

"I think you would," Mother said.

The next day at school Marina told Adam, "Today you can be my co-pilot. I'm going to be a pilot like that woman in the paper who has her own plane."

"What woman is that?" Adam said.

"Oh, I guess you didn't see her picture," Marina said. "Her plane has people in it and everything. Even her mother and father fly in it with her."

"Who is the stewardess in that plane?" Adam said.

"In the back there's a little machine and you get your own drinks by putting in some money," Marina said.

"That sounds like a good idea," Adam said.
He let Marina be pilot. He was co-pilot
and read the map and told her where to go.
There was almost a crash landing, but Marina
landed in a grassy field and everyone
got out safely.

The Way It Is

That afternoon their teacher read them a story about a king and queen. They had long red robes and had yellow crowns on their heads.

On the way home in the bus Marina said, "How about being a king? Or a queen?"

Adam thought about that for a minute. "No."

"You could have a red robe," Marina said. "You could have a crown."

Adam shook his head. "I wouldn't like that. Anyway, kings and queens don't do anything anymore. It would be dull."

"Maybe that's true," Marina said.

"What I'd like to be," Adam said,
"is president. That's better than being a king."

"President of what?" Marina wanted to know.

"Just president."

"You mean THE President?" Marina said.

"That's right," Adam said.

"What would you do if you were president?"
Marina asked.

"Oh," answered Adam, "I would sit
in a big room with a rug on the floor and
a big desk and I would sign papers and
everyone would have to do whatever I said."

"Maybe tomorrow we can play President,"
Marina said.

"O. K.," Adam said.

"Only, the thing is," Marina said, "what would
I be while you were president?"

"You could be my wife."

"What would I do if I were your wife?"
asked Marina.

"Well, you could make supper and get
the newspaper ready when I got home,"
Adam said.

"Sometimes you could ride in a car with me.
We could wave at people and they would throw
confetti at us."

"That sounds like fun," Marina said,
"only, Adam —"

"Listen," Adam said. "One thing I know.
There's never been a woman president."

That night after supper Marina said to her
mother and father, "I don't know what we're going
to do with Adam Sobel. He says such silly things."

"What did he say today that was so silly?"
her father said.

"He said there never was a woman president,"
Marina said.

There was a pause.

"Isn't he a silly boy!" Marina said.

"Well, it's true, there's never been
a woman President of the United States,"
Mother said.

"Other places have had outstanding women
leaders," Father said.

The next morning Marina said to Adam,
"Adam, you know, you can be a pilot or a doctor.
You know what I'm going to be?"

"What?" Adam said.

"I'm going to be the first woman President! . . .
You can be my husband."

"What would I do?" Adam said.

"You would fly our plane and fly me from place
to place so I could give talks," Marina said.

"From what you say, it seems like girls
can be anything they want," Adam said.

"Well, that's just the way it is now,"
Marina said. "Will you fly me to where I can
give my talk?"

"O. K., but after you give your talk,
you have to fly me back so I can give my talk,"
Adam said.

"O. K.," Marina said.

So Adam flew the plane to where Marina
had to give her talk, and she gave it.

Then Marina flew Adam to where he had to give
his talk, and he gave it.

Then there was a big Presidents' supper
with hot dogs, cheese, milk, cookies, pop,
and candy bars.

Both Presidents thought it was delicious.

Todd has lost nine pets.
Can you help him find them?

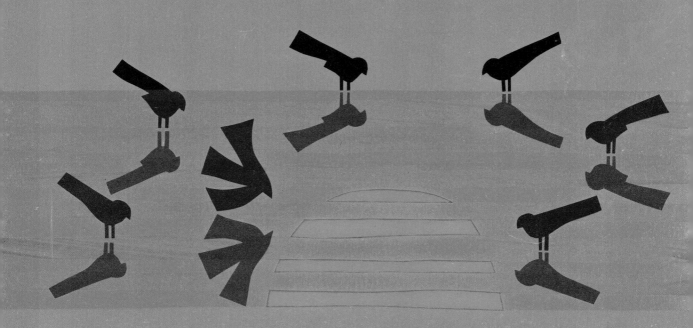

High Tide

Twelve Years, Twelve Animals

by Yoshiko Samuel

A long time ago in Japan, King decided
to ask all the animals to a party. He told them
to come to his castle on Saturday afternoon.

The animals were very happy to be asked,
and by Friday they were all hopping and running
with excitement! Tiger growled and growled
so the king would hear his best growling.

Dragon puffed smoke and said to himself, "I am sure King will be pleased to see how I do my tricks." Rabbit straightened his whiskers.

Dog cleaned his coat. Snake was ready for an exciting snake dance. Ox and Sheep practiced singing together until they couldn't sing any more. They could hardly wait for the big party day to come.

But poor old Cat! He just could not
remember when the party was going to be given.
So he went to his friend Mouse and asked him,
"When are we going to a party at King's castle?"

Mouse, who was almost always kind and
friendly, was feeling mean that day.
His bad teeth were making him cross.
So, without looking at his calendar,
he said to Cat, "Sunday will be the fun day."

On Saturday all the animals, but Cat, marched together to the castle. Mouse, with his bad teeth all taken care of, was riding on Ox's head and led the march. After Ox came Tiger, Rabbit, Dragon, Snake, then Horse, Sheep, Monkey, Rooster, and last of all, came Dog and Boar. It was a noisy, happy march.

King's castle stood tall and strong.
Its white walls looked bright in the sunlight,
and its turrets shined.

Castle guards met the animals at the front
door. They bowed politely to the animals
to show their welcome and opened the door.
The animals bowed politely to the castle guards
to show their thanks and then marched
right into King's party room.

King welcomed each of the animals
with a polite bow. He liked Tiger's
friendly growling and Rabbit's whiskers,
so fine and straight, and thought Dog had
the shiniest coat he had ever seen.

Then King asked everyone to a table filled
with food. On the table were candy and fruits
and lots of other delicious things to eat.
There was tea to drink, too.

All the animals had fun playing games,
eating fine food, and talking to one another.
King watched Snake's dance and listened happily
to Ox and Sheep sing. And when Dragon puffed
some smoke, King said to himself, "I am pleased
to know how Dragon does his tricks."

Everyone wished the party would last forever. But time went quickly, and soon the animals had to leave. So they all thanked King for the wonderful time they had and marched together back to their homes.

King walked outside. He looked at the moon shining on the water, and the twelve animals marching toward their homes. He felt very happy inside.

King said to himself, "From now on I will call each year with the name of an animal. Then I will be able to remember all twelve of the good animal friends who came to my party. I will call this year the Year of the Mouse, for Mouse came first. Next year will be the Year of the Ox, for Ox came second. And I will call the twelfth year from now the Year of the Boar, for he was the last one of the animals in the march. And then I will start again with the Year of the Mouse."

Poor Cat! The animals' noisy homecoming
woke Cat, who could tell they had all been
to King's party. He was angry at Mouse
for telling him the wrong day. Later, when
he found out that each of the animals who
had been to King's party would have a year
named for him, he was very angry. That is why
Cat and Mouse do not get along well to this day.

Even now, Japanese people call each year
with the name of an animal. I was born
in the year of the Tiger. In which year
were you born?

Here is how you find out:

1960	the Year of the Mouse	1972
1961	the Year of the Ox	1973
1962	the Year of the Tiger	1974
1963	the Year of the Rabbit	1975
1964	the Year of the Dragon	1976
1965	the Year of the Snake	1977
1966	the Year of the Horse	1978
1967	the Year of the Sheep	1979
1968	the Year of the Monkey	1980
1969	the Year of the Rooster	1981
1970	the Year of the Dog	1982
1971	the Year of the Boar	1983

A New Kind of Zoo

The Wild Animal Park in San Diego, California, is a new kind of zoo. The animals there do not live in cages. They live outdoors on open land.

Many of the animals at the Wild Animal Park come from East Africa. The land around San Diego is very much like their homeland. It is warm all year, and it doesn't rain much. The animals are able to live much the same way they would live in Africa.

Many animals in the park live together.
Some animals are kept by themselves so they won't
hurt other animals. The lions are kept in a
deep hole called a pit. The pit is very wide,
and the lions have a lot of room. But they
cannot get out of the hole to hunt other animals.

There are no cars in the park. Everyone rides on a train which goes through the park. This train is called a monorail. The monorail is not noisy, and it doesn't scare the animals. Everyone can easily see the animals through the monorail's big open windows.

It's fun to visit a zoo like the San Diego Wild Animal Park. It's interesting to see wild animals living outdoors. And it's good to know that the animals are free to move around on a lot of land.

THE PORCUPINE

The porcupine is puzzled
that his friends should act so queer,
for though they come to visit him
they never come too near.

They often stop to say hello
and pass the time of day,
but still the closest of them all
stays many feet away.

He sits and ponders endlessly,
but never finds a clue
to why his close companions
act the distant way they do.

The porcupine has never had
the notion in his brain
that what he finds enjoyable
to others is a pain.

Jack Prelutsky

Do You Have the Time, Lydia?

by Evaline Ness

Once there was a little girl named Lydia.
She lived with her father, who had a flower shop,
and Andy, who was her brother. Their house
was on an island.

Every day Lydia's father was busy
in his greenhouse, where the plants and flowers
got so tall they needed holes in the roof.

Every day Lydia was busy painting pictures,
reading books, building things, finding seashells,
and making cakes. Lydia was so busy doing
so many things she never finished anything.

Andy didn't do anything because he didn't
know how to. If he asked Lydia to help him
do something, she always said, "No-no-no-no!
I haven't got time!"

Whenever her father heard Lydia say that,
he always said, "Oh no? Oh ho! If you take time,
you can have time."

But Lydia was too busy to listen.

One bright morning, as Andy skipped
along the beach, he found an old lobster trap.
He dragged it home and into Lydia's room.
She sat sewing a dress for the cat.

"Look!" he shouted. "A racing car! Please,
oh please, Lydia, fix it for me so I can be
in Dr. Arnold's race! The prize is a dog!"

Without looking up, Lydia said, "No-no-no-no!
I haven't got time!"

"The race is this afternoon!" cried Andy.

Lydia stopped sewing long enough to look
at the trap. "Well, all right. I'll fix it,"
she said. "But later."

"You don't care!" cried Andy.

"I said I'd fix it, didn't I?" said Lydia.

Andy looked at Lydia for a long time.
Then slowly he backed out of the room.

Lydia dropped the cat's dress. She found
her skates and pulled them apart. She tied
each skate part to the four corners of the trap.
Then she cut two big paper circles
and put them on the front for headlights.
She took her doll's suitcase,
dropped everything in it onto the floor,
and placed it in the trap for a driver's seat.

"Great!" said Lydia. "All it needs now
is a steering wheel, and I know just where
to find one!"

Lydia ran to the garage. In one corner,
on a table, was a pile of old things.
At the very top was a doll carriage with one
wheel. As Lydia started to climb on the table,
she saw a big bowl on the floor.

"All that needs," said Lydia,
"is a little water and a few little fish.
And I know just where to find them!"

Away Lydia raced — through the pine trees
and down to the boathouse to get her fishing net.

The first thing she saw there was her father's
boat nearly filled with water. Lydia tried
to tip over the boat. It wouldn't move.
She found a can in the boathouse and started
to take out the water. But the more
she took out, the more water came in.
Lydia threw the can away and ran up the beach
toward the greenhouse to tell her father.

Take Time — Have Time

Halfway there, Lydia stopped. Near the water
was a sea gull. Its eyes were closed
and one wing was hurt.

"You need a doctor!" shouted Lydia.
"And I know just where to find one!"

She began to run. She ran so fast
she had run out of breath by the time
she reached Dr. Arnold's house. But Dr. Arnold
wasn't home. On the door was a note:
BACK IN 10 MINUTES. JUDGING RACE.

The race!

Up the street Lydia ran. At the top of the hill
she came to a sudden stop. There stood Andy,
alone. The race was over. All the cars were
at the bottom of the hill, and Dr. Arnold
was just giving a spotted dog to the winner.

Andy looked at Lydia. There were big tears
in his eyes. Then he turned and ran.

"Andy!" cried Lydia. "I was fixing it,
but I didn't have enough time!"

Andy kept running. He didn't look back.

Lydia watched him until he turned a corner.
Then she walked back to Dr. Arnold's house.
She sat down on the doorstep and cried and cried.
Then she stopped, because she had no tears left.

Suddenly someone said, "Well!
Have you finished your crying?"

Lydia looked down and saw Dr. Arnold's shoes.
Then she looked up and saw Dr. Arnold's face.
Between two sniffs Lydia said, "I guess
I did take time to finish something."

Dr. Arnold patted Lydia's head.

"Now what?" he asked.

Then Lydia remembered the sea gull.

"The sea gull!" she shouted. "Dr. Arnold! It's hurt. It's on the beach. It can't fly!"

"Hurry!" she called, as she ran ahead to the beach.

At last they were there, and there was the sea gull.

Dr. Arnold gave the gull something to make it sleep. Then he fixed its broken wing.

"This bird is going to be just fine," said Dr. Arnold. "But it won't be able to fly for a few days. Why don't you take the gull home, Lydia, and feed it a nice fat fish? That is, if you have enough time."

Lydia looked down at the sleeping sea gull.

"Oh ho! I'll take time!" said Lydia.

After Dr. Arnold left, Lydia took
the gull home.

She put seaweed around the bottom
of the basket. Then she carefully
placed the gull on its cool wet bed.

Lydia went looking for Andy. She found him
under the porch.

Lydia brought the sea gull in its basket
and placed it in front of Andy.

"Andy," said Lydia. "Look what I found
for you. It will be real when it wakes up.
You can have it all for your own."

Andy looked at the gull. He said nothing.

"Did you know that dogs can't fly?" asked Lydia.

Without looking at Lydia, Andy said,
"I don't want your old bird."

Lydia left the sea gull with Andy
and went back to the garage. She climbed
on the table and pulled off the carriage wheel.

As she was leaving the garage, Lydia spotted a birdhouse that she had started to make a long time ago. All it needed was a roof.

"What that birdhouse needs — " began Lydia. She stopped. She looked at the wheel in her hand. " — is nothing!"

Lydia raced out of the garage and into the house to her room.

She had just finished fixing the wheel into place when someone said, "I don't want your old trap."

"Oh, Andy!" cried Lydia. "Yes, you do, too! I'll paint it red and put a bell on it and it will be a fire truck, and you can go all around town and put out fires and help people!"

There was a long pause.

"Will it have a ladder?" asked Andy.

"A ladder, too!" cried Lydia. "I promise! I promise!"

"But you don't have enough time," said Andy.

"Oh no? Oh ho! If I take time, I can have time!" said Lydia.

maggie and milly and molly and may

maggie and milly and molly and may
went down to the beach(to play one day)

and maggie discovered a shell that sang
so sweetly she couldn't remember her troubles,and

milly befriended a stranded star
whose rays five languid fingers were;

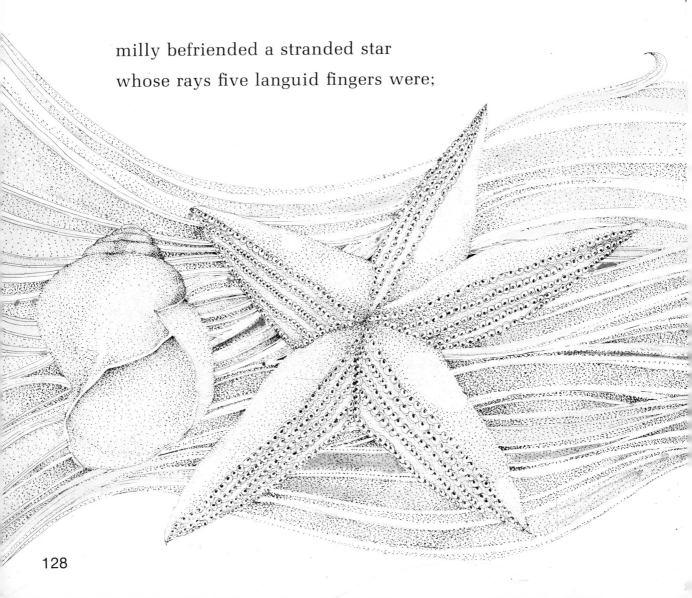

and molly was chased by a horrible thing
which raced sideways while blowing bubbles: and

may came home with a smooth round stone
as small as a world and as large as alone.

For whatever we lose (like a you or a me)
it's always ourselves we find in the sea

e. e. cummings

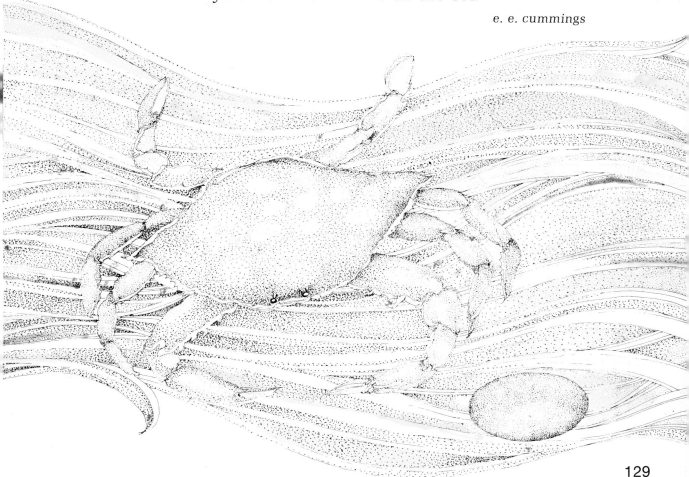

Vowel Sounds and Syllables

You know that the letters *a, e, i, o, u,* and sometimes *y* are called vowels. You also know that each of those vowels may stand for some vowel sound, like the short *a* sound in *cat,* or for no sound at all, like the *e* in *time.*

As you say these words to yourself, listen for the sound that each vowel stands for:

behind   garden   rocky

When you say those words, you say each one in two parts, like this:

be hind   gar den   rock y

There is just one vowel sound in each part. Each part is called a **syllable.** There are as many syllables in a word as there are vowel sounds in that word.

Say these words to yourself and think how many vowel sounds you hear in each:

angry problem grandfather umbrella

How many vowel sounds do you hear in *angry?* In *problem?* How many syllables are there in each of those words?

How many vowel sounds do you hear in *grandfather?* In *umbrella?* How many syllables are there in each of those words?

Say these words to yourself:

sat yet fix hot rug why

How many vowel sounds do you hear in each of those words? Each of those words is a one-syllable word. Each has just one vowel sound in it.

HAVING A PROBLEM WITH YOUR UMBRELLA, GRANDFATHER?

Sometimes a word has more than one vowel in it
but only one vowel sound and one syllable.

Say these words to yourself:

gave   rain   seek   coat

How many vowels are there in each of those words?
How many vowel sounds do you hear in each word?
There is only one syllable in each of those words
because there is only one vowel sound in each.

As you say each of the following words
to yourself, count the vowel sounds you hear
and decide how many syllables it has:

FLY AWAY.
YOU'RE FREE.

cat	**woke**	**second**
machine	**animal**	**afternoon**
boathouse	**candy**	**certain**

The WIZARD of WALLABY WALLOW

by Jack Kent

The Wizard of Wallaby Wallow was very busy.
He was trying to get his magic spells in order.
  He had spells for turning people
into everything from an anteater to a zebra.
Each spell was in a little bottle with a label on it
which told what kind of spell it was. But
everything was so mixed up that it took
the wizard hours to find the one he wanted.
So he took all the bottles off the shelves
and was very carefully putting the spells back
in alphabetical order.

The spells for turning people into anteaters,
ants, and antelopes went on the shelf labeled "A."
Bears, bees, and buffaloes went on the "B" shelf.
And so on.

"I wonder what kind of spell this is,"
said the wizard, looking carefully at the bottle
he had just picked up. "The label has come off."

Just then there was a knock on the door.
"Oh, horse feathers!" cried the wizard. "I'm
never left alone long enough to get anything
done."

He opened the door and said, "Go away.
I'm busy. SHOO!"

But the visitor was a mouse and used to having
people shout shoo at him, so he didn't much care
what the wizard said to him.

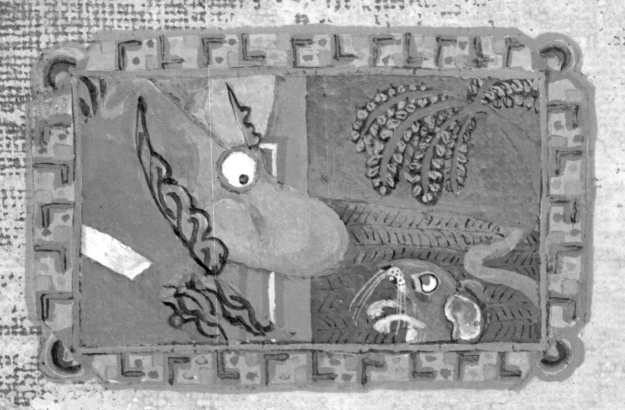

"I want to buy a magic spell," the mouse said.
"I'm tired of being a mouse. Nobody likes mice.
They set traps for us and get cats after us
and shout shoo at us. It's not a very easy life.
I want to be something else."

"Like what?" asked the wizard.

"I haven't decided," said the mouse.
"I thought I'd come and see what kinds of spells
you had and choose one."

"Everything's out of order right now,"
said the wizard. "Come back tomorrow and . . .

"Wait a minute!" he said, remembering
the bottle in his hand. "Here. You can have
this one. It's free." And he handed
the bottle to the mouse.

"There isn't any label on it," said the mouse.
"What will it turn me into?"

"Something else," said the wizard. "That's
what you said you wanted to be!" And
he banged the door and went back to putting
his spells in order.

WHAT WILL I BE ?

The mouse went home and set the bottle
on the kitchen table. While he was looking
for something to take the cap off with,
he tried to guess what the magic spell
would turn him into.

A butterfly, maybe? Butterflies are pretty,
but they don't live very long. He'd just as soon
not be a butterfly.

Turtles live a long time, but they aren't
very pretty. And they're so slow. The mouse
hoped he wouldn't turn into a turtle.

Bees are fast. But they work very hard.
Work was not one of the things the mouse
most liked to do.

Ants go on picnics. But ants get stepped on.

Birds sing happy songs. But birds eat worms.
The thought made the mouse a little sick.

"What if I turned into a cat!"
the mouse thought. "Cats eat mice!"
He turned white at the thought.

"Or what if it's a spell for turning people
into mice? On me it wouldn't even show.
It would be like dropping egg on a yellow bib!"
"Now, if I turned into an elephant,
that would be worthwhile," thought the mouse.
"But an elephant couldn't fit in my house."

It was a nice little house. The mouse
loved it very much. He hoped he wouldn't
turn into an elephant.

In fact, he couldn't think of anything
the spell might turn him into that he was sure
would make him happy.

"Being me has its problems," he decided,
"but at least I know what they are. Whatever
I turn into might have bigger ones."

So he took the magic spell back to the wizard.

The wizard came grumbling to the door.

He was still upset from putting the bottles
in order. He didn't recognize the mouse at first.

"You've changed," the wizard said.

"I may have," said the mouse. "I wasn't
a very happy mouse before. And now I'm . . .
well . . . something else."

"Was it the magic spell that changed you?"
asked the wizard.

"In fact, it was," said the mouse.

The wizard was so excited he could hardly
talk. "That's the first time one of my spells
ever worked!" he said delightedly.

"Looks like it worked two times,"
said the mouse. "It made us both happy.
It's a wonderful magic spell!"

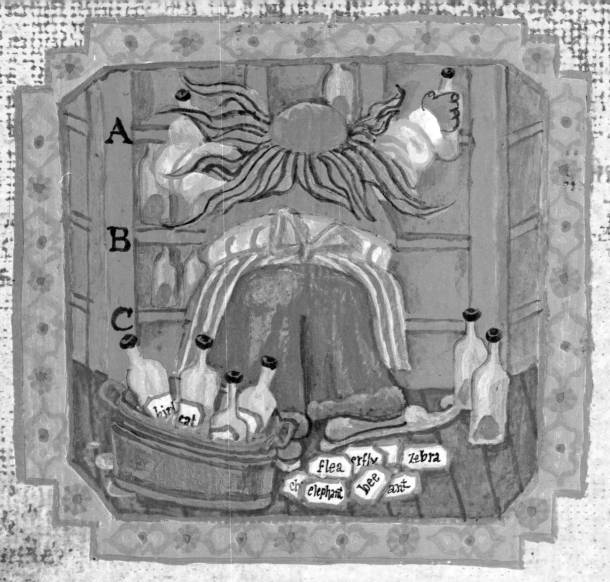

The wizard went into his shop and took
the labels off all the bottles and made
the prices higher. Then he put them back
on the shelves just any which way.

Putting them in order was no longer a problem.

Two Common Syllables

You know that a syllable in a word is a part that has just one vowel sound in it. Often we add one or more syllables to one word to make another word.

Look at the words in heavy black letters in these sentences:

1. I **wonder** if she'll say, "The show was **wonderful.**"

2. If you **help** others, they may sometime be **helpful** to you.

3. A **real** lion wouldn't **really** surprise him.

4. There was a **sudden** loud crash and **suddenly** it started to rain.

5. "Are you always that **slow?**" she asked as I climbed **slowly** up the tree.

What was added to the first word in heavy black letters in each sentence to make the second one?

WONDERFUL SHOW.

HELP!

I'M A REAL LION.

REALLY?

YOU'RE SLOW.

How many vowel sounds do you hear in *wonder* and *help*? How many do you hear in *wonderful* and *helpful*? Did adding the letters *ful* add another syllable each time? Did adding *ly* to *real, sudden,* and *slow* add a syllable? How do you know?

Look at *beautiful.* That word was made by adding *ful* to the word *beauty.* What happened to the *y* when the *ful* was added? When *ful* or *ly* are added to words that end with a *y* coming right after a consonant, the *y* almost always is changed to an *i.* See if you can tell what these words are:

busily   heavily   angrily   hungrily

Syllables like *ful* and *ly* added to words to make other words are sometimes called **common syllables.** You know the sounds that *ful* and *ly* stand for in a word. When you meet a word in your reading that ends with either one, think the right sounds for those letters. Also decide what the word looked like before that syllable was added. Doing those two things will help you in your reading.

146

Often you'll find *ful* or *ly* added to a word you know very well. Sometimes you'll find the two syllables together added to a word you know.

See if you can read the words in heavy black letters in these sentences.

6. That's a very **colorful** picture.

7. I wish you'd try not to be so **forgetful.**

8. Do you try to be **thoughtful** of the rights of others?

9. Ann is almost always smiling and **cheerful.**

10. Bob's dog is a very **friendly** one.

11. She loved her new pet **dearly.**

12. We take one newspaper that's only a **weekly.**

13. Have you seen Bob around here **lately?**

14. We're still waiting **hopefully** for her to say that we can go.

COCK-A-DOO-DLE-DOO.
IT'S ALMOST TWO.

WE'RE STILL WAITING.

HOPEFULLY.

MAYBE YOU CAN GO AT TWO.

THE QUEEN'S SCHOOL for PRINCES and LITTLE LADIES

147

A Window

A window:
a place to look
and see the beautiful trees,
a place for wind and air to
come and go as they please.
Most of all a window is
a picture hanging on my wall.

David Bears Heart

RED FOX AND THE HUNGRY TIGER

ANTELOPE

BUFFALOES

TUSKY PIG

RED FOX

LONG CLAW

BROWN BEAR

by Paul Anderson

Time: One day long ago

Place: In the jungle

STORYTELLER: The paw print of a tiger is as big as a man's hand. Yet, with his big paws, he walks so quietly that even the birds do not hear him as he moves through the grass. A tiger is big, bigger than a man, but a tiger is not easy to see in the jungle. When he stands still, even a rabbit will not know that he is there.

Little tigers like to eat four or five times each day. A big tiger doesn't get hungry that often, but when he does, he wants a lot to eat.

STORYTELLER

A dinner for an old tiger may be almost any animal. Because of this, a tiger does not have many friends. No one wants a friend who might forget and eat him for dinner when he is very hungry.

That was the way it was with a tiger named Long Claw. The only friend that Long Claw had was Red Fox. They were not really good friends, but they talked to one another.

LONG CLAW: I'm so hungry! I've looked for something to eat for three days. I want a big dinner! I wish something good would come along.

STORYTELLER: At the same time Red Fox was walking through the woods, Long Claw was waiting for something to come along that he could catch to eat.

LONG CLAW: What are you doing here? I can't catch anything if you come along and scare everything away.

STORYTELLER: Red Fox was scared. He knew how dangerous it was to make Long Claw angry when he was hungry. He just stood and shook.

LONG CLAW: Look here, I am very hungry. And because you came along while I was waiting to get something to eat, I'm going to eat you!

RED FOX: Oh, Mr. Tiger! You wouldn't eat me, would you? I am your friend, your good friend.

LONG CLAW: Friend or not, I must have something to eat this minute!

STORYTELLER: Red Fox knew that there was no help for him if he couldn't think of a plan. Now you know that foxes are very clever and so, in a minute, Red Fox knew what to do.

RED FOX: I don't think that you dare to eat me!

LONG CLAW: Dare to eat you! And why in the world shouldn't I dare to eat you?

RED FOX: Because, even though I am a small animal, I am a very dangerous one. All the other animals know this. They dare not touch me, even with their little finger claws.

STORYTELLER: This made Long Claw Tiger laugh.

LONG CLAW: Afraid of you? Think of anyone being afraid of a little thing like you.

RED FOX: You say animals are not afraid of me? I will just have to show you. Then you will believe what I have said.

Now, Long Claw, let us go for a walk through the woods. Follow me closely and you will see for yourself how everyone runs from me.

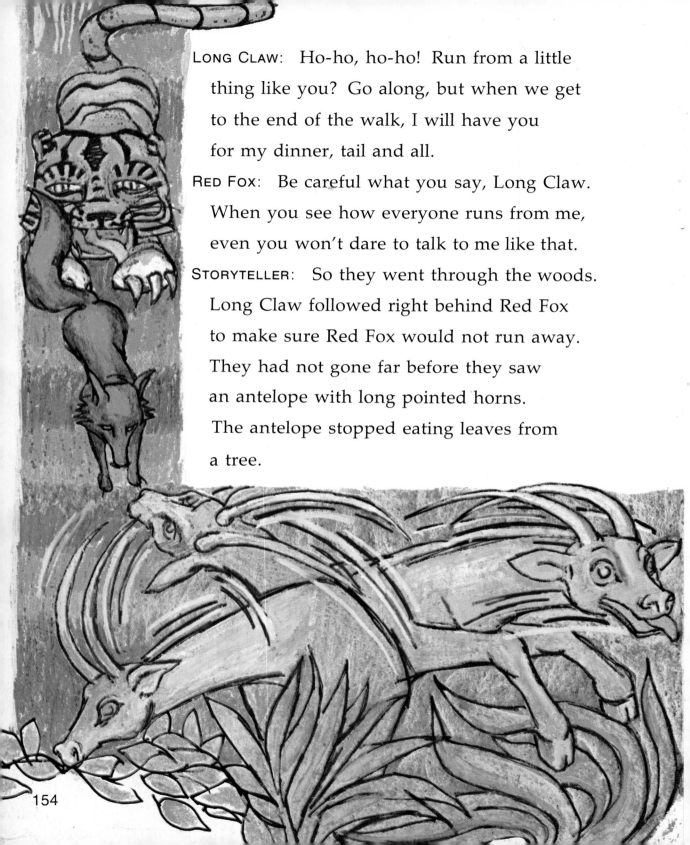

LONG CLAW: Ho-ho, ho-ho! Run from a little
thing like you? Go along, but when we get
to the end of the walk, I will have you
for my dinner, tail and all.

RED FOX: Be careful what you say, Long Claw.
When you see how everyone runs from me,
even you won't dare to talk to me like that.

STORYTELLER: So they went through the woods.
Long Claw followed right behind Red Fox
to make sure Red Fox would not run away.
They had not gone far before they saw
an antelope with long pointed horns.
The antelope stopped eating leaves from
a tree.

ANTELOPE: Look who's coming! E-h-h! Let me out of here.

RED FOX: There! Didn't I tell you? The minute Antelope saw me, he was terribly scared and ran away as fast as he could.

LONG CLAW: Well, well, well! He did. He sure did. But after all, he was only an antelope.

RED FOX: Wait and see.

STORYTELLER: Pretty soon they came upon a big brown bear eating berries from a bush.

BROWN BEAR: Help! It's you! You won't get me. WOOF! WOOF!

RED FOX: Aha! See how Brown Bear runs as soon as he sees me coming? I told you.

LONG CLAW: Well, of all things. I never would have believed it. That bear must have been sick.

RED FOX: Let's keep going.

STORYTELLER: Now Red Fox was enjoying his walk. He could see that Long Claw was really puzzled.

By and by, they came to a place where a wild pig was digging for fallen nuts. Tusky Pig was so busy digging that he didn't hear them coming.

When they came close to Tusky Pig, Red Fox gave a sharp bark.

Tusky Pig: Oh no! I'm getting away from here.

Storyteller: Tusky Pig turned and ran through the woods. He ran so fast he smashed down the bushes and tore through the trees.

Long Claw: Well, of all things! I never would have believed it! What makes them so afraid of you? You are not much bigger than a chicken. Your teeth aren't as big as the teeth of a little tiger. Yet, Tusky Pig runs away when he sees you. I just can't understand it.

Red Fox: I've never told anyone and I never will. Come on. Let's keep going.

157

STORYTELLER: They came to a river where two big water buffaloes were standing in the mud.

BUFFALOES: It's him! Run! Run for the woods!

STORYTELLER: They got out of the mud as fast as they could and went tearing off into the woods.

RED FOX: Well, what do you think now?

LONG CLAW: Think? I think I had better leave you alone! That's what I think.

STORYTELLER: Without another word, Long Claw ran through the woods as fast as he could without once looking back.

Red Fox lay down in the woods and laughed and laughed and laughed.

RED FOX: If a tiger's mind were only as sharp as his claws, oh my!

Parking Lot

Ten cars parked in a parking lot.
Some can run and some cannot.
Number one is out of gas.
Number two has broken glass.
Number three has lost its tires.
Number four has missing wires.
Number five is new and bright.
Number six has lost a light.
Number seven's all stripped down.
Number eight has rusted brown.
Number nine is engine-free.
Number ten belongs to me.

Marci Ridlon

159

Giraffes

I like them.
Ask me why.
    Because they hold their heads so high.
    Because their necks stretch to the sky.
    Because they're quiet, calm, and shy.
    Because they run so fast they fly.
    Because their eyes are velvet brown.
    Because their coats are spotted tan.
    Because they eat the tops of trees.
    Because their legs have knobby knees.
    Because
    Because
    Because. That's why
I like giraffes.

                    Mary Ann Hoberman

160

And Hippos Too!

Broad and heavy as a bus,
The cheerful hippopotamus
Is often seen to doze and float
Quiet as a drifting boat.
Almost nothing of him shows
Except his ears and eyes and nose.

His mouth, when opened hopefully,
Is a tremendous thing to see.
His tusky teeth and fleshy smile
Recall the cunning crocodile.
But really, hippo isn't snappy,
A simple peanut makes him happy.

Eunice de Chazeau

161

Following Directions

You can make a hand puppet of Little Hippo. All you have to do is to read these directions carefully and do exactly what they tell you to do.

First, ask your mother for an old, clean sock.

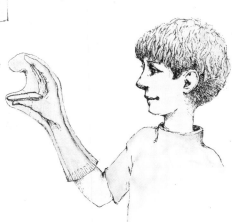

Then get some cardboard and cut this shape out of it:

Make it the right size to fit the heel of the sock.

Put it into the heel of the sock.

Now put your hand into the sock, like this:

You have made Little Hippo's mouth!

Put buttons on the top of the sock for Little

Hippo's eyes and nose, like this:

Then use two small rubber bands to make ears

for Little Hippo, like this:

You can make other puppets in much the same way.

If you read directions carefully and follow them

exactly, you can find out how to make or do many

things.

THE SECRET

A secret! A secret!

I just heard a secret

And nobody else must hear.

    No talking!

    No telling!

    No whispering!

    No hinting!

Or a secret will disappear.

A secret! A secret!

I just heard a secret!

Must it be kept so well?

    A week?

    An hour?

    A minute?

    A second?

I'm afraid I'm going to tell.

Leland B. Jacobs

Moon Glow

Moon Glow

The Case of the Stolen Code Book

by Barbara Rinkoff

The new boy sat on his back porch steps
watching the children play in the next yard.
He knew their names, but they didn't know his.
He had just moved in.

"Hi," he called and grinned at them
over the bushes in the yard. He grinned
whenever he talked to people.
It was a thing he did.

The girl called Winnie looked up,
but she didn't say, "Come and play."

The boys called John and Alex
stopped playing for a minute and stared.
John whistled through his front teeth,
and Alex looked over the top of his glasses.
But they didn't say, "Come and play."

The smaller girl, Hollie, sat
cross-legged next to her little dog, Panic,
and gave a little wave. But she didn't say,
"Come and play."

Panic, the little spotted dog, barked.

The new boy watched Winnie take out
a small black book.

"Meeting of the Secret Agents come to order,"
she said. She was a very businesslike girl.

And the new boy could tell they were having
a club meeting. But no one said,
"Come and play," to him.

The Secret Agents were very busy
using the small black book. The new boy
wanted to see it, too. But whenever he tried
to move from his porch steps, Panic barked.

When the children left the yard, they forgot the small black book. So the new boy went over and picked it up. There was no name on the cover, so he opened the book. Inside, it said: SECRET AGENTS' CODE BOOK in big red letters. The new boy grinned. He liked codes. Then he had an idea.

Soon Winnie, Alex, John, Hollie, and Panic
came looking for the small black book.

"I put it here, but now it's gone,"
said Winnie crossly. She knew losing
the Code Book was not very businesslike.

They searched all over. All they could find
was a blank piece of paper.

"Do you think it means anything?"
Hollie asked.

"Is it really blank?" asked Alex.

"Of course. I know writing when I see it,
and I don't see it," said Winnie.

John grabbed the paper and whistled
through his front teeth while he looked it over.
Hollie stood on tiptoe to look.
Alex came closer and looked, too.
Panic made a loud noisy yawn.
"Nothing there. Nothing at all," said John.
"Nothing . . . unless . . ." began Alex.
"Unless what?" asked Winnie.
"Unless it's in secret writing."
"Secret writing?" the others said.

"Maybe it's a clue," said Alex, cleaning his glasses on the tail of his shirt.

"A clue for what?"

"For our missing Code Book, of course."

"How?"

"Maybe the writing is invisible."

"What's invisible?" asked Hollie.

"You can't see it," said John.

"If you can't see it, what good is it?"

"Well, you can see it, if you know how," said Alex. He knew the most about magic and tricks.

"Then how?" asked Winnie, Hollie, and John. "It's not in our Code Book."

Alex went to the garage and put on
the wall light.

"You hold the paper next to the light,"
he said.

"I don't see anything," said Hollie.

"There's nothing there, that's why,"
said John, and he began to whistle through
his teeth again.

"Hey!" shouted Winnie.
"The paper is burning."

"No," said Alex. "Whoever left this note
wrote it in milk."

"Are you trying to tell us a cow left it?" asked Winnie. She liked things to be clear.

"No," said Alex. "Someone left us this note written in milk. To read it, we heat it with the light, and the writing will come out in brown letters."

And sure enough, there in front of them
was a message. It said:

To Find
Your book
here's where
To Look,
try Panic's
favorite bed.

"Where is that?" cried Winnie.

"Follow me!" called Hollie, racing across
the yard.

The Search Goes On

Hollie crawled into the doghouse, but
she couldn't go far. The opening was too small.

"You look in, John. You're the thinnest."

John put his head into the doghouse.
Panic sniffed at him.

"Nothing there but an old bone," said John,
throwing it across the grass.

Panic began to bark.

"Sh," said Hollie.

"Sh," said Winnie, John, and Alex. "We're thinking."

"You sure this is Panic's favorite bed?" asked Alex. "Where else does he sleep?"

Hollie thought a minute.

"Sometimes under my bed."

"Is that your favorite bed, Panic?" asked Winnie.

Panic began to bark again.

Hollie, Winnie, John, and Alex ran
for the house. They went straight
to Hollie's room. They searched under her bed.
There was nothing there but a fluff of dust.

"No book," shouted Hollie.

"No nothing," said John, and he began
to whistle.

"Wrong bed," said Alex.

"What other bed is there?" asked Hollie.

"A flower bed?" said Winnie.

Out of the house they ran, and, sure enough,
there was Panic digging away in the flower bed.

"Here's something," cried John, holding
a piece of paper.

As he opened it, they all looked. It said:

20-15   6-9-14-4   25-15-21-18

2-15-15-N   20-1-11-5

1-14-15-20-8-5-18   12-15-15-11

20-18-25   20-8-5   15-1-11

"Someone's using our Code Book," shouted Winnie.

"He sure is!" said John.

"Let's try to read the message," said Alex.

"Let's see. A is one. B is two. C is three."

"Oh, write it out, or it will take all day."

Winnie took out a paper and wrote:

And they all read:

To find your
book take
another look
try the
oak

"The oak tree!" Hollie shouted, and led them
across the yard, with Panic running close behind.

There, squeezed into a hole in the tree bark,
was another note.

"Here it is," shouted John.

"Read it," cried the others.

John opened the note. It looked very strange.

"What does that mean?" asked Hollie.

"Search me!" said Winnie.

"What good would that do?" asked Hollie.

"It could be one kind of mirror writing," said Alex.

"Mirror writing?" said the others. "It's not in our Code Book."

"Get me a mirror and I'll show you," said Alex.

Hollie ran back to the house to get one.

"You stand the mirror in front of the letters, like this," said Alex, and they all stood around him in the backyard watching him do it.

Then they read:

"Who's Bob Cox?"

Not one of them knew.

"I am," the new boy shouted across the bushes from his yard. "And here's your book."

He held it out to Alex.

"Well!" said Winnie.

"Well!" said Hollie.

"Well!" said John.

"Not bad. Not bad at all," said Alex,
and he smiled over his glasses as he took
the Code Book.

"You took our Code Book!" the others said,
pointing their fingers at Bob.

"I thought we could have some fun," he said.

Winnie, Hollie, John, and Alex looked
at each other.

"How'd you like to be
in the Secret Agents' Club, Bob?"
they all said together.

"Sure I would!" said the new boy, grinning
his biggest grin. "And you can have
all my secrets for our Code Book!"

CODES and SECRET MESSAGES

These people are trying to read a secret message that has been written in code. They cannot read it because they do not have a copy of the code in which it was written. When a message is written in code, the one who writes the message must have a copy of the code. The one who reads the message must also have a copy of the code.

There are many different kinds of codes you can use in writing secret messages. The pages that follow tell about some of them.

number Codes

In some codes a number is used in place of each letter. Here is one code that uses numbers:

A = 26	H = 19	N = 13	T = 7
B = 25	I = 18	O = 12	U = 6
C = 24	J = 17	P = 11	V = 5
D = 23	K = 16	Q = 10	W = 4
E = 22	L = 15	R = 9	X = 3
F = 21	M = 14	S = 8	Y = 2
G = 20			Z = 1

Can you read this message?

24-26-13   2-12-6   24-12-14-22   21-12-9

8-6-11-11-22-9

You can make up your own code with numbers. If you make up your own code, remember to use a *different* number for each letter of the alphabet.

Letter Codes

In some codes a different letter is used to stand for another letter. A code like this can be fun to make up and use. Here is one code that uses letters:

A = N	H = U	N = A	T = G
B = O	I = V	O = B	U = H
C = P	J = W	P = C	V = I
D = Q	K = X	Q = D	W = J
E = R	L = Y	R = E	X = K
F = S	M = Z	S = F	Y = L
G = T			Z = M

Using the letter code here, can you read this message?

TBYQ VF UVQQRA URER

191

Picture Codes

Here's another code that is fun to make up. Think of a different picture for each letter of the alphabet, like this:

A = □	H = ⊗	N = ◎	T = ☉
B = ◐	I = ▲	O = ▥	U = 〒
C = ⊞	J = 〓	P = ☼	V = ◖
D = ◑	K = ⧖	Q = ▽	W = ◒
E = △	L = ◉	R = ⊗	X = ⊜
F = ◣	M = ●	S = ◠	Y = ⊏
G = 8		Z = 🜍	

Using the picture code above, can you read this message?

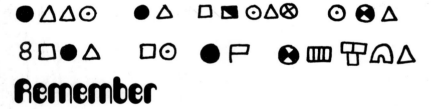

Remember

When you make up a code and write a secret message to a friend, always do these three things:

1. Use a different number, letter, or picture for each letter.
2. Give a copy of your code to your friend.
3. Keep a copy of your code for yourself.

Stickball,

Kickball,

Lickety-split ball.

   PLAY STREET — AREA CLOSED

No grass — black tar.

No cars, so far.

Beep! Beep! Spoke too soon.

"Get a horse, you big baboon!"

   PLAY STREET — AREA CLOSED

Can't he read?

Can't he see?

The sign says that this street's for ME!

   PLAY STREET — AREA CLOSED

Lee Bennett Hopkins

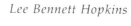

193

GABRIELLE and SELENA

by Peter Desbarats

Gabrielle and Selena went everywhere together. They did everything together. Although they had lived in the world for eight long years, they couldn't remember a time when they had not been together. They were like sisters.

Gabrielle seemed to know what Selena was thinking, and sometimes Selena would know what Gabrielle was going to say even before she said it. If Gabrielle started to say, "Why don't we ask your mother for some —" Selena would shout, "ice cream!"

Gabrielle had long hair that was almost blond.
She had green eyes, like the eyes of a kitten.
Often she was quiet, as if she were dreaming
about something or looking at something
far away that no one else could see.
But she wasn't always quiet.

Selena had short black hair. She had
big brown eyes. If you took a bowl
made of dark wood and filled it with rainwater,
that was the color of Selena's eyes.

Selena could do many things, but the thing
she did best and most often was laughing.
When she laughed, everyone else laughed too
and felt happy.

But sometimes she was quiet.

One hot day, when they were sitting on Mr. Mayer's front steps, halfway between Gabrielle's house and Selena's house, Gabrielle said, "Sometimes I wish, Selena, that I were you."

"Why do you want to be me?" asked Selena.

Gabrielle put her head in her hands. "I'm tired of being myself," she said. "Every morning I wake up in the same room, look at the same sister, say hello to the same father and mother, brush the same teeth, eat the same breakfast, and read the same newspaper, and —"

Selena looked at Gabrielle and said, "You don't read the newspaper."

"Sure I do," said Gabrielle, "I read it every morning just like my father does."

"What did you read about this morning?" asked Selena.

"I was in a hurry this morning, and I didn't have time," said Gabrielle. "Anyway, every day I do all these same things, and I'm tired of them. I think it would be more interesting to live at your house."

"But it's the same at my house," said Selena. "I always wake up in the same room and look at the same brother and eat the same breakfast and drink the same tea and —"

"You don't drink tea," said Gabrielle.

"Sure I do," said Selena.

"This morning?" asked Gabrielle.

"I was in a hurry this morning and didn't have time," said Selena. "Anyway, I do almost the same things that you do every day."

"But you don't do them just the same," said Gabrielle. "It would be much more fun if I could be you and you could be me."

"That's silly," said Selena.

"No it isn't — it's magic," said Gabrielle.
"All we have to do is put our hands together,
like this, and put our feet together, and put
our noses together, and I'll look into your eyes,
like this, and . . ."

Selena started to laugh. "Your eyes look funny,"
she said. "They look like one big eye
in your forehead."

"Stop fooling or it won't work," said Gabrielle.

"Now we turn around once, and I say — I am Selena."

"And I say — I am Gabrielle," said Selena.

They each took two steps backward and looked at each other.

"Hello, Gabrielle," said Gabrielle.

"Hello, Selena," said Selena.

"Well," said Gabrielle, "it's almost time for supper. I'd better hurry. Good-by, Gabrielle. Have fun at my house. I mean, your house."

"Good-by, Selena," said Selena. "Don't forget to feed my cat. I mean, your cat."

At Selena's House

When Gabrielle reached Selena's house, she rang the doorbell. Selena's mother opened the door and said, "Hello, Gabrielle."

"I'm not Gabrielle," said Gabrielle. "I'm Selena."

"Oh, I see," said Selena's mother. "Well, Selena, I don't understand why you rang the doorbell. Selena always just walks into the house."

"I forgot," said Gabrielle, and she walked into the house.

Selena's little brother was on the floor
in the living room, looking at a book.
"Hello, Gabrielle," he said.

"I'm Selena," said Gabrielle.

"O. K.," he said. "But you sure look
like Gabrielle, Selena."

Selena's mother came into the living room.
"Wash your hands, Selena," she said. "It's
time for supper. And we're having one of
your favorite things — turnips."

"Turnips are one of my favorites?"
asked Gabrielle, who couldn't stand them.

"Certainly they are," said Selena's mother.
"You always have two helpings."

"Ugh!" said Gabrielle to herself.

At Gabrielle's House

When Selena reached Gabrielle's house,
she walked right in. She went into the kitchen,
where Gabrielle's mother was standing in front
of the stove, and said, "What's for supper?"

"Oh," said Gabrielle's mother, "are you
staying for supper, Selena?"

"Of course I am," said Selena, "and
my name's Gabrielle."

Gabrielle's mother turned around and looked at her. "Where's Gabrielle? I mean, where's Selena?" she asked.

"Selena's at my house," said Selena. "I mean, her house."

"Very well, Gabrielle," said Gabrielle's mother. "Wash your hands for supper. We're having your favorite — a great big omelet."

"That's my favorite?" asked Selena.

"I always give you an extra-big helping,
and you always come back for more," said
Gabrielle's mother.

"Ugh!" said Selena to herself, because
if there was one thing she couldn't stand,
it was an omelet. She didn't like eggs —
any kind of eggs, and an omelet was about
the most horrible thing you could turn an egg into.
It tasted like wet newspaper to Selena.

Somehow Selena ate most of her supper.
When it was time for dessert, there was cake
for Gabrielle's mother and Gabrielle's father
and Gabrielle's little sister — who kept
calling her Selena — and bread and butter
for Selena.

"Where's my cake?" said Selena.

"Why, Gabrielle, you know you never eat cake,"
said Gabrielle's mother. "You always say
that the best dessert in the world is bread
and butter."

"I do?" said Selena.

Back at Selena's House

When Gabrielle had finished most of her turnip, trying to look as if she liked it, Selena's father said, "Now it's time to clear the table and do the dishes, Selena."

"But I haven't had any dessert," cried Gabrielle.

"Why, you know we always have ice cream
for dessert on Thursday, and you don't eat
ice cream," said Selena's father just as a big
helping was put in front of him.

"I don't?" said Gabrielle.

"Never!" said Selena's father. "You haven't
eaten ice cream since your last party,
when it made you sick."

"Maybe I'd like it now," said Gabrielle.
"Maybe I could try a little bit."

"I don't think that's a very good idea," said Selena's father, putting a big spoonful of ice cream into his mouth. "If it made you sick, you couldn't wash the dishes."

"Wash the dishes?" said Gabrielle. "But I always watch TV after supper."

"I don't know what you're talking about, Selena," said Selena's mother. "You never watch TV. You always say it's much more fun to wash the dishes."

After Dinner at Gabrielle's House

At Gabrielle's house, Selena was sweeping the kitchen floor. Gabrielle's mother had said that this was what she did every night before she went to bed at eight.

"You mean I have to go to bed at eight?" asked Selena.

"You don't have to. You want to go to bed early," said Gabrielle's mother. "Every time I ask you to watch TV with me, you say that it's much healthier to go to bed early."

"Well!" said Selena to herself. "No wonder
Gabrielle wanted to be me. Omelets. Sweeping
the kitchen. Going to bed at eight. No TV.
This is a terrible way to live."

Then she looked up at Gabrielle's mother
and said, "I'm going home."

"All right, Selena," said Gabrielle's
mother, laughing.

After Dinner at Selena's House

At Selena's house, Gabrielle had just finished
the dishes when Selena's father said, "Time
for bed, Selena."

"But it's only eight," said Gabrielle.

"Is it that late?" said Selena's father.
"My! My! By this time you're sound asleep
on the back porch."

"The back porch?" said Gabrielle.

"You always say that it's healthy to sleep
outside," said Selena's father.

"But it's dark out there and cold,"
said Gabrielle.

"I know," said Selena's father, "but that's the way you like it. I don't know how many times you've said that you like sleeping on the cold back porch and looking at the stars, much more than you like being in a nice bedroom."

"Boy!" said Gabrielle to herself. "I never knew that Selena was such a nut. Turnips. Washing the dishes. Sleeping on the back porch."

Gabrielle looked up at Selena's father and said, "I'm going home."

"All right," said Selena's father, smiling. "Good night, Gabrielle."

Together Again

Gabrielle and Selena met on the sidewalk under the streetlight in front of Mr. Mayer's house.

"Hello, Selena," said Selena, looking at Gabrielle.

"Never mind calling me Selena," said Gabrielle. "I wouldn't be you for all the money in the world. You didn't tell me that you liked turnips."

"Turnips?" said Selena. "I can't stand turnips. But you didn't tell me that you loved omelets."

"Ugh!" said Gabrielle. "I hate omelets almost as much as I hate washing dishes."

"But you sweep the kitchen floor every night," said Selena.

"I do not," said Gabrielle, "and I don't sleep on the back porch."

"Who sleeps on the back porch?" cried Selena.

"But your father said —" said Gabrielle.

"And your mother said —" said Selena.

Suddenly the two little girls looked
at each other and started to laugh. And
their laughter sounded in the night like bells
    ... under the streetlights
         ... under the stars
              ... under the quiet black sky.

Getting to Know Story Characters

Most of the stories you have read are about people or animals. We call them story characters.

The sentences below tell about a character named Alfred. What do they tell you about him?

LET'S READ ABOUT ALFRED.

> A boy named Alfred said good-by to his mother and started down the street for school. At first he walked right along, but then he slowed down. Pretty soon he met another boy who was also on his way to school.

Those sentences tell only a little bit about Alfred. They tell you that he's a boy. What else do they tell you about him? Do they tell you anything about the feelings he had as he went to school?

Most of the time, a story will tell you enough about the characters so that you can really feel that you know them. It will tell you more than you found out about Alfred in the sentences above.

Following is the first part of a story
about Alfred. As you read it, find out all you
can about Alfred.

Today was the first day of school! Alfred put on the new red sweater his grandmother had sent him.

"Mom, I'm ready for school," he said.

"I'm sure you'll have a good day," said his mother. "Remember how nice Miss Larkin seemed when we talked with her?"

"Good-by, Mom," called Alfred, as he skipped down the walk and started off.

Soon, though, he slowed down and began to walk much more slowly. He thought, "I wonder if I'll like the new school. I won't know any of the other boys and girls. I wonder if they'll be friendly or if they'll make fun of me and laugh at me."

Just then he saw a boy staring at him from the street corner up ahead. "Hi!" the boy called. "My name's Jim. Let's walk to school together."

"Hi!" said Alfred. "My name's Alfred and we just moved here."

"I know," said Jim. "My mom told me you're going to be in my room at school."

"That's wonderful!" said Alfred with a big smile. "Now I'll know someone before I even get there."

I'M GLAD THAT ALFRED MET JIM.

Now you should know much more about Alfred. Was Alfred happy when he started for school? How do you know? How did Alfred feel just before he saw Jim? Why did his feelings change after he met Jim? What else did you find out about Alfred?

Did you notice how you found out about how Alfred felt and why? The story didn't say that at first he was excited and happy. But you knew he was because he skipped down the walk. How did you know he was a little scared about going to a new school? How did you know he got over being scared? You could tell from what he thought and said and did, couldn't you?

When you read a story, look for what it tells you about the characters. Find out about those characters by noticing what they say and do. Doing that will help you understand and enjoy the story.

Now read the part of a story shown on the next page.

GOODBYE, ALFRED.

SAY GOODBYE TO ALFRED.

His hair was long and reddish-brown in color. He belonged to Mr. Sims, but all the children on the street played with him. He'd sleep all day on the front steps until the children came by on the way home from school. Then he would open his soft brown eyes. His big ears would go up and his long, fluffy tail would begin to wag.

"Hi, Big Red," the children would call out as he ran to meet them.

What did you find out about the character those sentences tell about? How did you find out those things?

I FOUND OUT THAT BIG RED SLEEPS A LOT.

WHAT DID YOU FIND OUT?

CRADLE SONG

Coo . . . ah . . . coo . . . !
Little Dove,
Coo . . ah . . coo!

The wind is rocking
Thy nest in the pine bough,
My arms are rocking
Thy nest, little Dove.

Coo . . . ah . . . coo
Little Dove
Sleep Little Dove
Coo . . oo . oooo Little Dove!

PAIUTE from a collection by
Mary Austin

FOLLOW THE WIND

by Alvin Tresselt

The wind blew for days and days. Nothing
could stop the wind, and nothing could follow
it to the end. Sometimes it was gentle
and sometimes it was strong, but it always kept
blowing.

As the wind moved along, it sang a little
song to itself:

"Oh, I am the wind and I do as I please.
I blow away dust and I blow away trees."

"I will follow the wind," said the kite.
"I will go to the end of the wind."

The kite sailed up higher and higher.
It sailed over the trees and the roof-tops
and almost up to the clouds.

But the kite came to the end of its string
before it came to the end of the wind.

"*HO HO,*" laughed the wind, and it blew on to a field of dandelions.

"We will float with the wind," said the white dandelion feathers when a little boy blew them. "We will go wherever the wind goes."

They danced on the air as the wind ran after them, around and around the little boy's head. But one by one they came down to the grass.

"*WHOOSH,*" went the wind, and blew off the little boy's hat.

"I will go with the wind," said the old windmill. "I will go as fast as the wind."

Slowly, the windmill started turning, then faster and faster as the wind grew stronger. But even though the mill went faster, it was always in the same place.

And the wind laughed:

"Oh, I am the wind and I do as I will.
I play with the kite or I work
with the mill."

"I will fly with the wind," said the little
bird, stretching its wings. "I will fly
to the end of the wind."

The little bird beat its wings faster
and faster. But the sky was so big and the wind
was so strong that the little bird grew tired.
It flew down to a tree to rest.

The wind shook the tree's branches
and went on.

"I will go with the wind," said the cloud. "I have no string to hold me and I have no wings to grow tired. I will fly across the great sky."

The wind blew harder and the fat white cloud hurried along with it for miles and miles. But soon the cloud grew bigger and bigger. It got so heavy that hundreds and hundreds of raindrops fell from it.

Then the wind cried:

"Oh, I am the wind and I blow the rain.
And when I blow hard, I'm a hurricane!"

And the lightning tore through the sky, and
the trees shook until the hurricane was over.

233

"I will sail with the wind," said the sailboat.
"I will go until there isn't any more wind."
   The white sail blew in the wind, and
the boat floated over the white-capped waves
past fishing boats and lighthouses. But it came
to the land before it came to the end of the wind.

"I will stop the wind," said the gruff old
mountain. "I stand so high over the land that
the wind will have to stop."

But the wind blew higher and higher,
up the side of the mountain, right over the top
of the topmost rock on the top of the mountain.
Then it hurried down through the woods
on the other side.

And nothing could stop the wind.

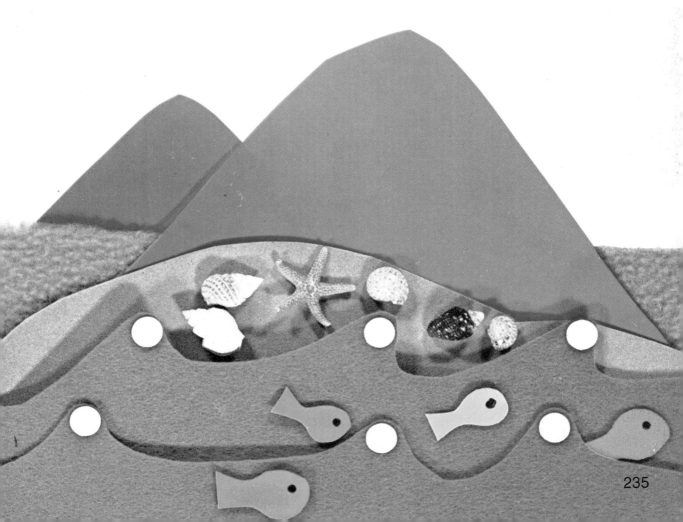

"I will reach the end of the wind," said
the airplane. "I will fly three times
around the world until I reach the end of the wind."

The airplane flew over mountains,
over rivers, and over seas, three times
around the world until it ran out of gas. But it
never reached the end of the wind.

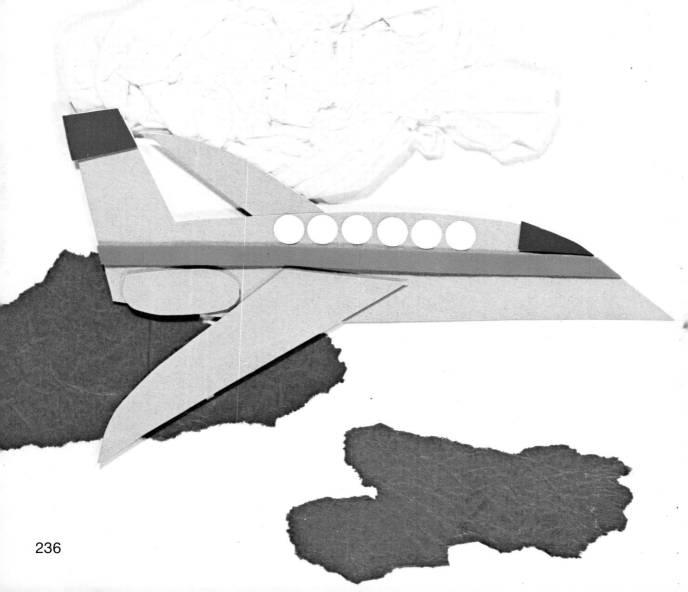

And the wind blew all over the world.

At last, after days and days, when the wind
grew tired of blowing and pushing birds and boats
and clouds and kites, it sang another song:

"Oh, I am the wind and I've been on a spree.
I've danced with the dandelions, ruffled the sea;
I've beaten an airplane and shaken a tree;
I did what I pleased, and they followed me!"

Then the wind grew gentler and gentler
and gentler as it rocked itself to sleep.

Spinning Song

The bar is smooth
    beneath our knees,
Our hands are strong,
    we sit at ease,
And when we're set
    we grab hold tight,
And back we spin
    with all our might.

The bar gets hot —
    around, around —
Our flying hair
    whips air and ground.

Of all who spin
    on playground bars,
We are the best!
    we are the stars!

238

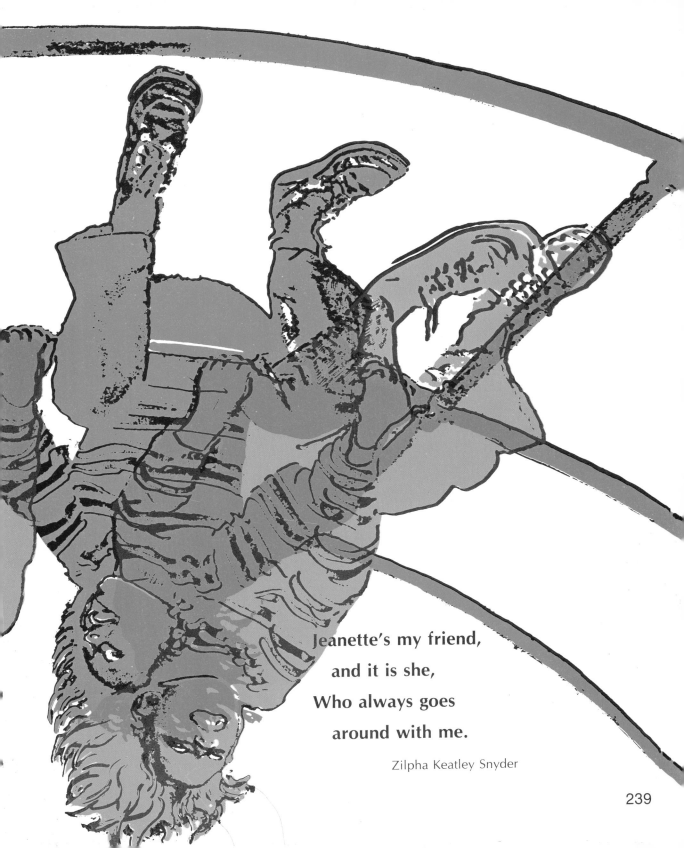

Jeanette's my friend,
and it is she,
Who always goes
around with me.

Zilpha Keatley Snyder

239

Getting the Setting of a Story

When you start reading a story, you want to find out — as soon as you can — when and where the things in the story are supposed to have happened. Then you can understand better why the characters do what they do.

If a story starts out "Once upon a time," what does that tell you about when the story happened? Does it make you think that the story happened a little while ago? A long time ago?

Very few stories start out with "Once upon a time" or even with something like "This happened in Kentucky in 1920." To find out when and where a story took place, you have to make use of what the story does tell you.

The sentences below are the beginning sentences of a story. What do they tell you that helps you know *when* the story took place?

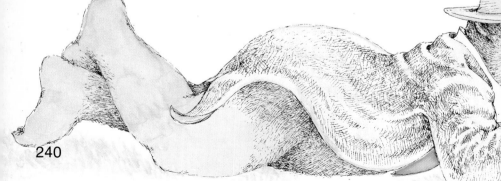

It was bitter cold outside, but the fire in the fireplace helped to warm the one-room house. Chad's father had made the house from trees he had chopped down. One fireplace couldn't keep even that one room very warm. The cool breeze blew through the walls of the room. Chad and his father and mother didn't mind because no one else around had anything more than a fireplace to keep them warm in those days.

Do you think the story took place a long time ago? Just a little while ago?

What kind of house did this family live in?

Why did they have only a fireplace to keep warm?

Which sentence helped you most to know when the story took place?

Below is the beginning of another story. What does it talk about that helps you know *where* the story happened?

Susan was all excited. Her mother had told her she could have the girl she'd met at her grandfather's come and visit them. Susan made all kinds of plans. Ellen could help her feed the chickens and bring in the eggs. She'd show Ellen the big barn and all of the cows and horses. She knew her father would let Ellen ride one of the horses. But best of all, she'd have a chance to see Ellen again.

I'M WAITING TO BE FED.

Where do you think this story takes place?

What sentences or parts of sentences helped you to know where the story took place?

When you find out *when* and *where* a story takes place, you are finding out about what is called the setting of the story.

As you read each of the next two story beginnings, try to decide what is the setting for each story.

> Bob and Betty liked riding down in the elevator. Riding down from their apartment was much easier than walking down five flights of stairs. Their apartment house was on a very busy street. They walked along past many stores and crossed two busy streets to get to the park. They found quite a few things to do there. First they were horses and galloped around. Then they bought some popcorn and tiptoed over to feed the pigeons. On the way home they watched the men working on a new apartment building — nineteen stories high!

Robbie would sit day after day down by the waterfront. He'd listen as some man shouted out orders and then watch the other men carry goods on board from where they were piled up on the docks. He liked to watch the big sailing ships and wished he could go away on one. He wished he could go and see that new land across the sea he'd heard about. One of his father's friends had gone to a new land called America.

I WISH THAT ROBBIE COULD HAVE COME WITH US.

AMERICA BOUND

Did You Know?

A snowflake always has six sides. But of all the snowflakes that fall, no two are ever exactly alike.

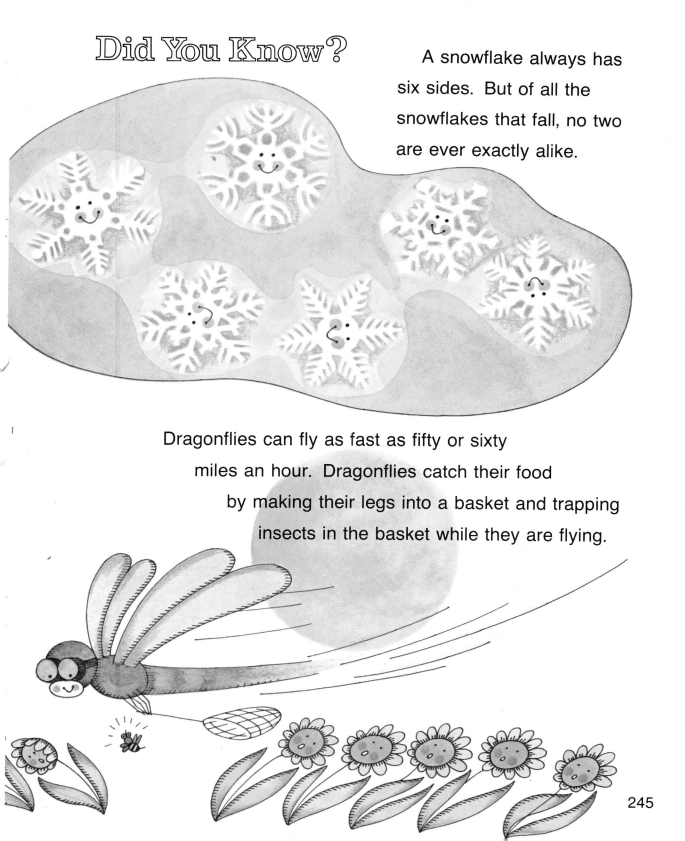

Dragonflies can fly as fast as fifty or sixty miles an hour. Dragonflies catch their food by making their legs into a basket and trapping insects in the basket while they are flying.

The ostrich is one bird that cannot fly, but it can run very fast. An ostrich can run faster than most race horses and sometimes men have races with them.

The elephant uses its trunk to have a drink. It takes water into its trunk and then squirts it into its mouth.

246

Impossible Possum

by Ellen Conford

Randolph was a little possum. His mother worried about him.

"I don't understand it," she said. "All possums hang by their tails and sleep upside down. Why can't you?"

"I don't know," Randolph said sadly. "I certainly try hard enough."

"Try again," said his father. "Maybe you just need more practice."

"All right," sighed Randolph. He crawled
out onto a branch of their tree, held on tightly,
and took a big breath.

"Don't look down," said his father.

"Don't be scared," said his mother.

"You can do it!" called his brother.

"No, he can't," said his sister.

Randolph curled his tail around the branch, took another big breath, let go with his paws, and hung by his tail.

"Good for you!" shouted his father.

"My boy's growing up," sighed his mother.

"You're doing it!" shouted his brother.

"No, he's not," said his sister, as Randolph's tail uncurled and he fell to the ground, head first.

"Oh, my!" said his mother. They all hurried
to help Randolph.

"Are you hurt?" asked his mother.

"No more than any other time," sighed
Randolph. "I don't think I broke any bones."

His father shook his head.

"I just don't understand it. Your mother
and I can hang by our tails. Your sister
Geraldine can hang by her tail.
It's the most natural thing in the world
to sleep upside down."

To show Randolph how easy it was,
Geraldine went back up the tree.
She ran out on a branch,
hung upside down, and sang
"Pop, Goes the Weasel!"
as she swung by her tail.

"Would you like to hear me
sing something else?" she asked.

"Nobody likes a show-off,"
said Randolph angrily.

"Why don't you try it again?" his father said.
"You almost had it that time."

"It's impossible," Randolph said. "I just
can't do it."

"Are you really trying your best?" asked
his mother.

"If at first you don't succeed, try, try again,"
said his father.

"Practice makes perfect," said his brother.

His sister didn't say anything, because
she was busy doing tricks while she hung
by her tail.

"It's just impossible," Randolph sighed.
"You might as well get used to it —
I just can't do it."

"Yes, you can," said his mother. "You
just have to keep trying."

"I *can't* keep trying!" cried Randolph.
"Every time I try, I fall on my head."

"If you didn't hurt your head all the time,
would you keep trying?" asked Eugene.

"I guess so," said Randolph. "But how
could I keep from hurting my head?"

"We could put a big pile of leaves under the tree," Eugene said, "so if you fall, you won't get hurt."

"*If* he falls! You mean, *when* he falls," said Geraldine.

"Never mind, Geraldine," said her father. "It's a very good idea. Now, go help your brothers get some leaves."

Randolph, Eugene, and Geraldine ran around picking up leaves until there was a big pile of them under the branch where Randolph practiced.

"Here I go again," said Randolph. He climbed up the tree and out onto the branch, curled his tail over the branch, and hung upside down. His tail uncurled, and he fell head first into the pile of leaves.

"Do the leaves help?" asked his mother.

"A little," said Randolph, as he climbed up the tree once more.

Again and again he tried to hang by his tail, and again and again he fell onto the pile of leaves.

They're Stuck

His brother and sister went off to play.
His mother went in to make dinner. His father
went for a walk.

Randolph kept hanging and falling.

At last he gave up.

"I have fallen for the last time," he said
to himself, as he lay on his back in the pile
of leaves.

"Maybe other possums can sleep upside down,
but I am different. When everyone else goes
to sleep and they all hang upside down
on the branch, I will sleep on my pile of leaves.
It's really nice enough here. In fact, I think
I'll go to sleep right now." And he did.

Randolph woke to find that Geraldine
and Eugene were jumping into his pile of leaves.

"Whee!" shouted Geraldine, "this is fun!"

"It may be fun for you," Randolph said sadly.
"For me, it's just a place to sleep."

He stood up and dusted himself off.
A few leaves stuck to his tail.

"I'll help you," said Eugene. He tried
to brush the leaves off Randolph's tail,
but they wouldn't come off.

"They're stuck on," he said.

"Don't be silly," said Geraldine. "How can
they be stuck?" She reached down and grabbed
a leaf off Randolph's tail.

"Ouch!" said Randolph. "That hurts!"

"Look!" Geraldine said. She pointed
to a very small branch halfway up the tree.
Something was slowly dripping from its end.

"Sap!" said Eugene. "You got sap on your tail
and it made the leaves stick!"

Randolph stopped pulling leaves from his tail.

"Why didn't I think of this before?" he cried
as he held his tail under the branch.

"If sap makes leaves stick to my tail,"
Randolph shouted as he raced up the tree,
"maybe it will make my tail stick to the branch."

Randolph curled his tail around the branch
and held on with his paws until he was sure
the sap was sticking. Then he let go
and hung down. He didn't fall.

"Look at me!" he shouted. "Look, everyone!"

Eugene began clapping. His mother came outside and watched, smiling happily. His father heard the noise and came running.

"He's doing it!" Eugene cried. "Randolph's hanging by his tail!"

"Good for you, Randolph," said his father. "You see practice does make perfect."

"I don't think it was the practice so much as the sap," Randolph said.

"Sap?" said his father.

"Oh, my," said his mother.

"I think it's very clever," said Eugene.

"I think it's cheating," said Geraldine.
"Anyway, how are you going to get down?"

"I never thought of that," Randolph said.

"Don't worry," his mother said kindly.
"We'll just unwind your tail for you
when you want to come down."

"Well, I think I'll just hang here for a while,"
said Randolph. "The world looks so different
upside down. The sky is on the ground
and the grass is up in the sky. It's very restful!
I might even have a little sleep."

He closed his eyes and fell asleep.

He's Doing It!

From then on, Randolph held his tail
under the sap before the possums went to sleep,
and his mother would unwind it for him
when he woke up.

But one day, Randolph noticed that the sap
had dried up.

"What will I do now?" he cried.

"Maybe you should try again
without the sap," said his father.

"It's impossible," said Randolph.
"I always fall on my head."

"Randolph," said his father, "winter is coming.
In the winter, sap dries up. You must try
to hang like the rest of us."

"Maybe we can find another tree with the sap
coming out," said Eugene, who didn't always
listen to his father. "I'll help you look."

So Randolph and Eugene went off together
to look for some more sap.

"It's impossible," said Randolph, after
they had been searching for some time.
"I guess Father was right."

Sadly, Randolph and Eugene
walked back home.

"I might as well start making another pile
of leaves," sighed Randolph. "I'll need
a place to sleep."

Just then, Geraldine came racing toward them.

"Look what I found!" she called. She showed
Randolph two wet leaves.

"I found some sap, and I put it
on these leaves," she said grinning. "Would you
like me to rub them on your tail?"

"That's very nice of you, Geraldine,"
said Randolph, and he held out his tail.

Then he ran up the tree.

"I hope you put enough on," he worried.

"Oh, I did," said Geraldine happily.

His mother and father came out when they heard him.

"Geraldine found some sap for me," Randolph said.

"What a good sister!" said his mother.

"It was nothing," said Geraldine.

"Look!" called Randolph, who was hanging by his tail. "It works perfectly. Thank you, Geraldine."

Suddenly Geraldine cried, "Randolph, you're doing it! Look at Randolph! He's doing it!"

"Of course he's doing it," said Eugene. "He can always do it with the sap on his tail."

"No, no, no!" cried Geraldine, hopping up and down. "It wasn't sap. It was water! I put water on the leaves. It was a trick!"

"Water!" cried Randolph.

"What?" said his father.

"Oh, my," said his mother.

"That was a dirty trick," said Eugene.

"But he *is* hanging by his tail!" Geraldine
kept saying. "By *himself*!"

"I am?" cried Randolph.

"He is!" said his father. "I'm certainly
surprised."

"Oh, Randolph, I'm so proud of you!"
said his mother, and she was so happy
she began to cry.

"I can do it! I can do it!" Randolph shouted.

"All you needed was a little confidence,"
said his father.

"And a tricky sister," said Eugene.

"You mean, a smart sister," said Geraldine.

The possums were so excited that they
ran out onto the branch and sang
"For He's a Jolly Good Fellow" to Randolph,
as he hung upside down by his tail.

And no one sang louder than Randolph.

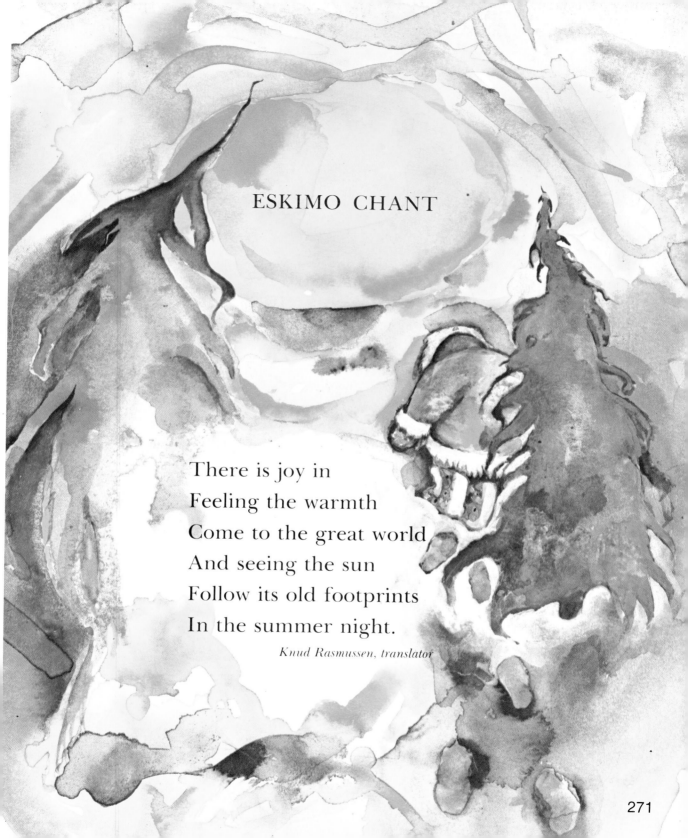

ESKIMO CHANT

There is joy in
Feeling the warmth
Come to the great world
And seeing the sun
Follow its old footprints
In the summer night.

Knud Rasmussen, translator

Illustrators: PP. 7–22, JOHN FREAS; PP. 27–38, TOM COOKE; PP. 40–41, DAVID MCPHAIL; PP. 42–43, MARC BROWN; PP. 44–63, JOHN KUZICH; PP. 64–66, DAVID MCPHAIL; P. 67, SAS AND ALISON COLBY; PP. 68–89, JAN PALMER; P. 90, TOM COOKE; PP. 93–105, LEONARD LUBIN; P. 109, RONALD LEHEW; PP. 110–127, EVALINE NESS; PP. 128–129, JIM SPANFELLER; PP. 130–132, DAVID MC-PHAIL; PP. 133–144, ERIC VON SCHMIDT; PP. 145–147, DAVID MCPHAIL; PP. 149–158, MICHAEL MILAN; P. 160, PEGGY GREEN-FIELD; P. 161, BOB BARNER; PP. 162–163, DAVID MCPHAIL; P. 164, CECILE WEBSTER; PP. 167–188, JOEL SNYDER; PP. 189–192, BOB BARNER; P. 193, BILL MORRISON; PP. 194–218, LARRY NOBLE; PP. 219–223, DAVID MCPHAIL; P. 224, CAROLE KOWAL-CHUCK; PP. 225–237, LOIS EHLERT; PP. 240–244, DAVID MC-PHAIL; PP. 245–246, IKKI MATSUMOTO; PP. 247–270, SUE THOMPSON; P. 271, CAROLE KOWALCHUCK.

Photographers: P. 23, ROBERT L. DUNNE (*top*), JOHN C. STEVENSON, ANIMALS ANIMALS ENTERPRISES © 1975 (*bottom*); P. 24, M. P. L. FOGDEN/BRUCE COLEMAN, INC. (*top*), RUNK/SHOENBERGER, GRANT HEILMAN PHOTOGRAPHY (*bottom*); P. 25, ZIG LESZCZYN-SKI, ANIMALS ANIMALS ENTERPRISES © 1975; P. 26, JOHN S. FLANNERY/BRUCE COLEMAN, INC. (*top left*), LEONARD LEE RUE III/BRUCE COLEMAN, INC. (*top right*); P. 39, ERIK ANDERSON; P. 106, SAN DIEGO ZOO (*top, and bottom left*); GEORGE S. SHENG (*bottom right*); P. 107, SAN DIEGO ZOO (*top*), GEORGE S. SHENG (*bottom*); P. 108, SAN DIEGO ZOO; P. 148, ERIK ANDERSON; P. 159, ERIK ANDERSON; P. 160, MARTUCCI STUDIO; P. 189, ERIK ANDERSON (*top*); PP. 240–241, BONNIE UNSWORTH.

Book cover, title page, and magazine covers by GERALD MCDERMOTT.

DEFGHIJ-D-843210/798